Dependency and its
Implications for Rehabilitation

The New England Regional Rehabilitation Research Institute

Reuben J. Margolin, Project Director
George J. Goldin, Research Director

Northeastern University Studies in Rehabilitation

No. 8 *Social Disadvantagement and Dependency: A Community Approach for the Reduction of Dependency through Vocational Rehabilitation*, by George W. Craddock, Calvin E. Davis and Jeanne L. Moore, 1970.

No. 9 *Structure and Dynamics of Social Intervention: A Comparative Study of the Reduction of Dependency in Three Low-Income Housing Projects*, by Gary Spencer, 1970.

No. 10 *Psychodynamics and Enablement in the Rehabilitation of the Poverty-Bound Client: An Approach to Reducing Dependency*, by George J. Goldin, Reuben J. Margolin, Bernard A. Stotsky and Joseph N. Marci, 1970.

No. 11 *The Rehabilitation of the Alcohol Dependent: An Exploratory Study*, by Sally L. Perry, George J. Goldin, Bernard A. Stotsky, and Reuben J. Margolin, 1970.

No. 12 *The Rehabilitation of the Young Epileptic*, by George J. Goldin, Sally L. Perry, Reuben J. Margolin, Bernard A. Stotsky, and June Foster, 1971.

Dependency and its Implications for Rehabilitation

Revised Edition

Northeastern University Studies
in Rehabilitation Number 13

George J. Goldin

Sally L. Perry

Reuben J. Margolin

Bernard A. Stotsky
New England Regional
Rehabilitation Research Institute
Northeastern University

Lexington Book
D.C. Heath and Company
Lexington, Massachusetts
Toronto   London

Social and Rehabilitation Service of the Department of Health, Education and Welfare reserves a royalty-free, nonexclusive and irrevocable license to reproduce, publish, and translate or otherwise authorize others to use this material, which was developed out of Grant 12-P-55011/1-04.

This study is based upon investigation supported by Grant number 12-P-55011/1-04, Social and Rehabilitation Service.

Printed in the United States of America

International Standard Book Number: 0-669-83949-3

Library of Congress Catalog Card Number: 72-1968

Table of Contents

vi

Bibliography

About the Authors

Preface

This book represents an expanded version of an initial monograph entitled *Dependency and Its Implications for Rehabilitation*, published by the New England Rehabilitation Research Institute at Northeastern University.

Few if any would disagree that client dependency is a variable which must be confronted by rehabilitation practitioners in all settings. Yet, many who are called upon to work with dependent clients have had little opportunity to become sufficiently familiar with the dependency literature for it to be helpful in their clinical work. The purpose of this book is to summarize relevant literature dealing with dependency, comment upon it, and point out its implications for the field. In addition to reviewing the literature, the senior author has set forth a typology for classifying dependency which, it is hoped, will be used by professionals in the field of rehabilitation.

Two major difficulties were encountered in writing this book. One stemmed from the conceptual difficulty encountered in working with dependency. The other difficulty concerned level selection. A highly theoretically-oriented work would be appreciated by rehabilitation psychologists and social scientists but would have little appeal for the practitioner in rehabilitation. On the other hand, a highly practical orientation would not necessarily command the interest of researchers and theoreticians. To resolve this problem we have attempted to achieve a balance between theory and practice in the hope that this book will have value for all interested in and working within the field of rehabilitation and social welfare.

Since the publication of the initial monograph there has been a burgeoning of interest in the problems of dependency and much has been written in this area. However, it should be pointed out that the major portion of research which has been done has involved children and college students who were essentially normal. There is a great need for dependency research with populations who suffer pathologically as well as populations who are socioeconomically disadvantaged.

The new vast literature on the subject of dependency made selection of relevant material difficult. Rationale for selection of articles to be reviewed for the revised volume was guided by an effort to include primarily those which were related to the functioning and adaptation of people within the various social systems which comprise their milieu. This does not imply elimination of studies carried out in a constructed experimental setting; however, these were necessarily limited in number.

Acknowledgments

Sincere thanks are extended to Mr. Neil Fallon, Regional Commissioner, Social and Rehabilitation Service, and his staff for their guidance and support.

This group of acknowledgments would not be complete without expression of our gratitude to William F. Fitzgerald, Dean of Academic Affairs and Vice President, Northeastern University. We are also indebted to Professor Martin E. Essigmann, Dean of Research, Northeastern University and his staff. Without the support, cooperation, and encouragement provided to the New England Rehabilitation Research Institute by these men this book could never have been written.

Our thanks go to Miss Mary Louise Young for her performance of the clerical tasks connected with this volume. Finally, we express our sincere gratitude to all the many readers of our first monograph on dependency who were kind enough to write to us, provide us with their helpful comments and encourage us to write this second volume.

Major Implications for Rehabilitation

The material discussed in the text of this book contains numerous implications for the field of rehabilitation and social welfare. In the section which follows, only the major implications are summarized.

1. Expressions of dependency differ and are related to factors in the particular milieu which precipitates them. This book groups dependent expressions in five categories: social, emotional, financial, institutional and psychomedical. While these expressions are related and similar, they must be dealt with by differing interventive techniques on the part of the rehabilitation professional.
2. Eriksonian theory is helpful in understanding and developing ways and means of coping with excessive client dependency. Basic trust and autonomy should be established and the client's identity reconstructed.
3. A knowledge in depth of the client's background is most important in coping with client dependency. Studies have suggested that certain variables, such as position in the family, parental rejection and restriction, etc., are associated with dependent behavior.
4. The relationship between dependence and suggestibility indicates that a certain amount of directiveness can be utilized by the rehabilitation professional with his dependent clients. However, since dependency is related to conformity, over-directiveness should be avoided.
5. Dependent individuals respond positively to rewards when selectively and discriminately used. However, dependent-anxious individuals perform less well under reward conditions. Increased anxiety mobilizes further dependency. Application of rewards with clients in rehabilitation centers and sheltered workshops should, therefore, be carefully evaluated and carried out with care.
6. Socio-cultural factors are important in the patterning of dependent responses. These factors can be either motivating or inhibiting forces in the rehabilitation process. The practitioner should consider ethnic and other subcultural attributes in formulating rehabilitation plans for his client.
7. Dependent individuals respond well to structured situations; lack of structure creates anxiety. The manipulation of the degree of group structure within rehabilitation settings, as well as the use of special group treatment techniques, offers an opportunity for the practitioner to reduce client dependency.
8. Peer group esteem has been found to be of much importance to dependent individuals. The use of group pressures to reduce dependency in rehabilitation clients merits further experimentation.
9. The rehabilitation practitioner must be alert for dependency conflict in his

clients. Behavior that appears to be highly independent may mask strong feelings of dependence. This conflict can take its toll in client anxiety, blocking successful rehabilitation.

10. More should be done in experimentation with operant conditioning techniques in the reduction of dependency in rehabilitation clients. This is an area in which further investigation might prove fruitful.

11. The theoretical material in the area of perceptual dependency offers a significant and fertile field of research for rehabilitation professionals.

12. The particular social system in which dependency occurs influences the manner in which it manifests itself in the rehabilitation client.

1

Theories and Concepts of Dependency

Client dependency, its management, and its reduction during the rehabilitation process present the professional worker with a complex and crucial problem. To ignore the client's dependent strivings is to run the risk of his feeling rejected and withdrawing. Yet, complete acceptance of such strivings by the practitioner entails the risk of fostering dependency and impeding the flow of the rehabilitation process.

Theories and Concepts

It is well known that regression into dependency is concomitant with the "illness state." Parsons (1965) went as far as to characterize the "sick role" as containing elements of social deviance deriving from the secondary social, emotional, and, in some instances, material gains attendant upon that role. In helping the disabled client emerge from his dependent state, rehabilitation fulfills two critical functions. It enables the client to achieve a higher level of personality integration for happier living and serves as a socially controlled means for the social and economic betterment of society in general.

Regardless of the setting in which the rehabilitation professional functions, or the aspect or phase of rehabilitation in which he is involved, dependency of the client remains a barrier which must be surmounted. It is, therefore, of paramount importance that professionals involved in the rehabilitation of the physically, mentally, and socially disabled acquire as much knowledge as possible about dependency and its correlates.

Dependency is as difficult to deal with conceptually as it is in actual practice. How can dependency be defined? Is it a personality trait or attribute? Is it a state related to situational factors within the subject's psycho-social milieu at a given time? If dependency is trait-like in character, is it a unitary trait or is it a configuration or constellation of factors?

Webster's dictionary defines dependency as "relying on or subject to something else for support; not able to sustain itself without the will, power, or aid of something else." While this definition is semantically helpful, it is highly limited as a psychosocial description of dependency. From a behavioral standpoint, dependency is an inherent component of human functioning. This is understandable when one considers that during his early years from birth onward the child cannot exist without adults to meet his primary needs

1

(psychological as well as physical). Stotsky (1963) described this dependent relationship as follows:

The human infant at birth is in a state of unconditional dependence upon others for its very existence and for the satisfaction of basic biological needs. Without the assistance and attention of an adult, the infant would perish. This is the prototype of a dependent relationship between one person and another.

As the infant enters childhood, he gradually learns to respond to other humans in a social and later in a symbolic manner. For the learning of these highly complex and abstract attitudes and behaviors, he is again primarily dependent upon parents; secondly on other members of his social environment. . . . A dependent relationship with a parent is a necessary precondition for socialization of the child.

However, the description, delineation, and measurement of dependency becomes a major task of vast complexity. Sears (1963) spoke of dependency as "one of the most significant, enduring, and pervasive qualities of human behavior. From birth to old age, it influences the form of all dyadic relationships." Although the term dependency is defined in varying ways, many behavioral scientists still view the concept in terms of succorance as elucidated by Murray (1938). His description of succorance involves demands for food, affectional nurturance, and the associated caretaking activities characterized in the mother-child relationship.

Further concepts such as tactile contacts as well as the "desire to be near" are also considered aspects of dependent behavior. The importance of tactile stimuli in the satisfaction of dependent and security needs in animals has been well substantiated by the studies of Harlow (1958). Moreover, the imprinting studies (Lorenz, 1957; Bateson, 1966; Jaynes, 1967, 1968) have demonstrated the instinctual attachments of the infants of a number of species to the first moving objects they see. Fleener's (1968) work demonstrated similar attachment formation in human infants. In her review of the theoretical literature on the development of infant-mother attachment, Ainsworth (1969) presented and evaluated psychoanalytic theories of object relations and social learning theories of dependency, then delineated an ethological approach to attachment which holds that infant-mother ties can be formed in the absence of primary drives and in the absence of conventional reinforcement. A comprehensive and impressive body of research supporting such an approach with implications for practice was presented by Ainsworth (1970).

Although the importance of the role of genetic and evolutionary factors in determining individual biases cannot be minimized, the individual is, nevertheless, subject to environmental influences both prior to and after birth. The contributions made by the psychoanalytic, learning, developmental, and sociocultural theories toward understanding the development of psychosocial dependency in the individual as he interacts with his environment will be presented.

Psychoanalytic Theory

Both psychoanalytically-oriented psychologists and learning theorists have been active in proposing causal hypotheses for dependency. Psychoanalytic theorists hold that inappropriate dependency arises from prolonged failure to gratify oral (food) and affectional needs of the child in his early years of life, particularly during the first year when major psychic energies are fixated on the oral erogenous zone. When such love is denied, the frustration produces a type of affectional void or vacuum which the individual attempts to fill by dependent demands. This dependent behavior satisfies the psychic economy in two ways. On the one hand, there is a gain that arises from the attention the individual receives as a result of his dependent demands. An additional gain accrues from the retaliative gratification which the person receives from the indirect expression of hostility through the manipulation of significant others in his milieu. On the other hand, over-gratification of demands during the early developmental period can increase expectations of oral demands being gratified and, in this way, heighten dependent strivings in the child.

The psychology of Erikson (1959) made an important contribution toward the understanding of the development of dependency. In placing Freud's psycho-sexual development stages in a social context, he depicts personality development in the individual as resulting from the manner in which the child copes with a series of epigenetic crises in the growth process. Thus, during the oral stages, described by Erikson as the stage of basic "trust vs. mistrust," a failure to trust the parent or parent figure as a source of warmth, food, and affectional gratification can produce dependent demands that result from the child's insecurity and need for reaffirmation of the positive relationship.

During the second or anal stage, which Erikson characterizes as the state of "autonomy vs. shame and doubt," the person's capability for independent functioning is also influenced. If parents do not allow autonomy to develop through the child's mastery of his sphincter and other muscular movements, the ensuing shame can cause doubt, feelings of inadequacy, and subsequent reluctance to undertake new and independent behavior. Erikson's description of the third stage (phallic) as one of "initiative vs. guilt" clearly indicates the potential for dependence or independence to develop as a response to the manner in which the child is allowed to express aggression and helped to deal with anxieties resulting from his budding genital sexuality and his oedipal conflicts.

Erikson's global concept of identity is useful in attempting to understand dependency. The individual whose identity is strong and intact has the security to function in a constructive and independent way. On the other hand, the person who suffers from identity diffusion has difficulty in mustering the ego strength to pursue sustained independent behavior. The recently published book, *Dependence in Man: A Psychoanalytic Study*, by Parens and Saul (1971), is noted for the benefit of those who are interested in the psychoanalytic aspects of dependency.

Learning Theory

Bandura and Walters (1959), in a book that explores aggressiveness in adolescence, have put forth a theory of dependency based on anxiety. They assume that dependency becomes a secondary drive: the presence of parents at times of reinforcement of primary drives makes parental attention a secondary reinforcement. When this secondary drive is frustrated by lack of attention or by punishment, the dependency drive becomes more intense and an aggressive drive will result. As the child learns to anticipate nonreinforcement of the dependency drive, dependent behavior becomes associated with anxiety. The anxiety, coupled with the increased dependency drive, makes the child's situation sufficiently upsetting to cause him to inhibit overt dependency behavior toward his parents. The aggression he feels toward his parents is displaced to other individuals who will not punish aggressive behavior.

Another behavioral theory, similarly based on anxiety, has been developed by psychoanalysts such as Horney (1939) and Sullivan (1953). Anxiety is said to result from experiences of negative reinforcement of independent behavior. Fear of further punishment makes a person quite reluctant to attempt independent behavior. Secondly, the dependent behavior is seen as a mechanism for reducing anxiety and achieving security. Dependency, then, is a learned neurotic response to fear of the prospect of independence.

Mowrer (1960) attempted to explain dependency in terms of the combination of the individual's reactions to the dependency drive. Since the person experiences both positive and negative reinforcements of the dependency drive, he is likely to feel both hope for a favorable response to his drive and fear of an unfavorable one. Whether or not a dependent response will occur depends upon the intensity of the drive at the moment. The conflict between the positive and negative expectations mediates the intensity of the drive and influences the occurrence of the response. As a result, dependent responses are less likely, yet are more extreme when they do occur.

These theories were presented and criticized in an article by Gavalas and Briggs (1966). The authors' primary objection was that a number of complex constructs were presented—dependency, frustration, aggression, anxiety, inhibition, displacement—which for two reasons did not readily lend themselves to research. First, the number of constructs employed to explain dependency was too large to permit isolation of a single factor. Secondly, each factor was too vaguely defined for the experimenter to establish a definite relationship. Since empirical evidence has not emphatically sustained or discounted any of these theories, a new concept of dependency, based on Skinner's paradigm of concurrent schedules of reinforcement, was proposed.

The theory proposed to alleviate this problem describes two connotations of dependency: the desire to be near people and behavior that does not seem appropriate to given occasions. It accepts the first step of the current theories—

that the simple presence of people acquires value as a secondary reinforcement. Second, independent behavior that is not reinforced becomes a discriminative stimulus for periods of no reinforcement. These two steps result in a strong habit of dependent response. The individual substitutes the secondary reinforcement of dependent behavior for the less distinct and often less immediate reinforcement of independent behavior.

Four concurrent schedules were established: reinforcement of independent behavior alone, of dependent behavior alone, of both, and of neither. Where both behaviors are reinforced and on a variable ratio schedule of reinforcement, they predict either fixating on one response, alternating between the two, or superstitious patterns. Where only one response is reinforced, only the reinforced response will appear. The authors also proposed that certain intrinsic reinforcements of independent behavior (e.g., task completion) would cause the extinction of independent behavior to be more difficult than that of dependent behavior. As the individual matures and specific reinforcements of dependent and independent behavior no longer regularly occur, independent behavior, during this period of extinction, will tend to increase its prevalence. However, since the dependent response may not be specifically extinguished, it might be recovered dramatically if in later life the individual is placed in a context of strong and frequent dependency reinforcement (e.g., a long hospital stay). Speer (1967) provided partial support for this concurrent schedules of social reinforcement model of dependency.

Some of the limitations the authors placed on their proposals include: 1) utilizing reinforcement schedules in a home would be difficult; 2) the intrinsic reinforcement of independent behavior is questionable; 3) the concept of secondary reinforcement is perhaps too broad; 4) the concurrent schedules consider only two alternatives—dependent and independent responses—and make no provision for other kinds of behavior resulting from the schedule. Murillo (1965) presented three conceptual models and some evidence suggesting that an approach-avoidance conflict conceptualization of dependency might prove more valid than either an approach or an avoidance model.

Learning theorists have, then, described dependency as a behavioral response which is acquired through reinforcement in much the same way as the more rudimentary behavioral patterns are learned. An individual initially responds at random in the presence of an unspecifiable stimulus. Through reinforcement the response becomes conditioned to that stimulus and is subsequently emitted by it. For example, a hungry infant cries in the presence of its mother. Repeated reduction of the infant's hunger drive by the mother will on future occasions evoke the infant's cry response when hungry. Physical contact, caressing and other attention behaviors which are present at the time the primary drive is reinforced become, themselves, through association, secondary reinforcers. Dependency as a learned response is thus created.

Let us suppose that a mother withdraws nurture from the child and positively reinforces independence while negatively reinforcing dependence. According to operant theory the child should, with a continuing of the reinforcement schedule, respond with independent functioning. However, psychodynamic theorists specify that, if such action occurs during the early biologically dependent phases of the child's development, it would constitute rejection or at least affectional deprivation and would cause the child to react with over-dependence. Such dependence would remain with the child as a high secondary drive, difficult to extinguish. On the other side of the coin, over-gratification of the child's dependent strivings past the weaning stage can also create over-dependency as a secondary drive which does not extinguish easily and requires little in the way of reinforcement. In other words, the etiology of dependency must be related to the time of life of the individual in which the dependency-producing stimuli occur. During the very early years of development, pressure for independent functioning, when basic survival depends on gratification by adults, may well be regarded as a deprivation and may result in inappropriately dependent, withdrawn, or narcissistic behavior. On the other hand, later in the life of the child, when independence is rewarded by society and dependence frowned upon, independence may be a learned response. A first basic question is at which point in life does the acquisition process of dependent behavior move through the transition from an essentially instinct-based response (hunger, etc.) to a socially conditioned response. A second process about which little is known is how the two types of acquisition (instinctual and social)blend and combine to produce the dependency component in the adult personality.

Developmental Theory

Although many aspects of dependent behavior may find their etiology in early childhood, the individual's capacity for independent functioning is reaffirmed or impeded during adolescence. It is during this period that the child makes his first major bid for the emancipation that will prepare him for independent adult functioning. This push for emancipation is not without its highly conflictive elements, since the adolescent yearns for the security of a dependent relationship with his parents while simultaneously feeling the need to compete independently and adequately with the members of his peer group. Some families are able to help their adolescent members through this emotionally turbulent phase while others are not. Conflict resulting from the search for independence during adolescence has been described by Eisenberg (1965). In his attempt to gain independence from the family, the adolescent tends to identify strongly with and obtain need satisfaction through his peer group. Conflict ensues, however, when the family cannot gradually relinquish its dominant role in proportion to the strides made by the adolescent toward independence.

Murphy et al (1963) explored the relationship between autonomy striving and parent-child patterns of interaction during the shift from high school to college. Both students and their parents were interviewed at strategic points during the transition period. By studying the student-parent relationship it was noted that autonomous behavior could be achieved either by gradually attaining independence while remaining close to the family or by attaining independence at the expense of close family ties. Parents who were able to delegate increasing responsibilities to the child, who were confident that the child had the ability to assume an adult role, and who could treat the child more or less as an equal remained close to their children. On the other hand, students who achieved autonomy at the expense of family ties had parents with a similar value system but in the final analysis these parents, unwilling to give up their dominant role, showed considerable inconsistency by treating the child sometimes as an adult and other times as a child. The resulting conflict, due to inconsistency of role expectation, forced the student to choose between a dependent parent relationship and self sufficiency, the latter choice occurring when the need for independence was greater than the need for dependence. Students not having achieved a suitable level of independence by the end of freshman year in college were judged by their parents as unable to deal adequately with the adult world.

According to Jones (1961), the transition from dependence in childhood to independence in adulthood depends primarily upon the redirecting of the infantile attachment of libidinal energy invested in the parent to that of a love object other than the parent. Thus, when the adult stage is fully realized, the adolescent is able to relinquish the incestuous attachment to the parent and obtain need satisfaction from the nonincestuous love object. In other words, independence is achieved when the need to be loved becomes subordinate to the need to love. In addition to defining dependency in terms of psychoanalytic concepts, Jones pointed to the possible misconception held by many that the infant feels helpless and defenseless. He stated that while it is true that the infant is dependent upon the parent for need satisfaction it does not necessarily follow that the infant perceives of himself as dependent. In fact, because he has not yet progressed to the level at which he can distinguish his own body from that of the external world, the infant is actually more apt to consider himself powerful than impotent. The basis for the misconception was said to lie in the projection by the adult of his own feelings of dependency.

Adolescence was characterized by Maier (1965) as a discrete phase, not a transitional one, in the developmental process. The phase itself, however, is comprised of a series of transitions from dependence to independence, each representing the attainment of a new level of self-sufficiency. In his rejection of parental dependency, the adolescent relies on his peer group for the fulfillment of many of his needs until such time as he is prepared to enter and assume the responsibility of the adult world.

Dependency, of course, is not confined to infancy, childhood, and adolescence; it can be found at any developmental stage of life. An excellent discussion of dependency among the aged can be found in *The Dependencies of Old People* (Kalish, 1969), in which several authors offer their views on dependency in later life. This work describes dependency in old age in terms of its psychological, medical, economic, cultural, and cognitive aspects.

Sociocultural Theory

Frequently dependency is spoken of as though it were a totally intrapsychic trait. While many of its manifestations convey this impression, the importance of cultural factors in conditioning dependency is clear. Ruth Benedict (1959) pointed this out most succinctly in comparing the childbearing practices of the culture of the United States with those of other cultures. She described the process in some cultures in which the child is prepared for an independent adult role from an early age by adults who motivate his participation in activities which will later be expected of him. In American culture, on the other hand, there exists a marked discontinuity between the frequently sheltered and over-protected existence of the child and his rather abrupt entry into the adult world where a great premium is placed upon independence, competition, and successful achievement. In commenting on this discontinuity Benedict remarked:

It is clear that if we were to look at our social arrangements as an outsider, we should infer directly from our family institutions and habits of child training that many individuals would not "put off childish things"; we should have to say that our adult activity demands traits that are interdicted in children, and that far from redoubling our efforts to help children bridge this gap, adults in our culture put all the blame on the child when he fails to manifest spontaneously the new behavior or, overstepping this mark, manifests it with outward belligerence. It is not surprising that in such a society many individuals fear to use behavior which has up to that time been under a ban and trust instead, though at great psychic cost, to attitudes that have been exercised with approval during their formative years. Insofar as we invoke a physiological scheme to account for these neurotic adjustments, we are led to overlook the possibility of developing social institutions which would lessen the social cost we now pay; instead we elaborate a set of dogmas which prove inapplicable under other social conditions.

It would appear that economic and demographic factors are causing the cultural conditioning of dependency to increase rather than decrease. In our early, essentially agricultural economy and rural society, children were compelled to begin participating in the earning of a livelihood at an early age. Later, as industrialization and urbanization took place, young people were thrown into the teeming competitive environment of the city where independence was, in a sense, tantamount to social and emotional survival. However, with the advent of suburban movement, middle- and lower-class parents adopted a more pampering attitude toward their children. Since distances between home and destinations are greater than in the city, children are frequently chauffeured to activities. Most leisure time activities for children and youth are programmed so that little in the way of self-initiated behavior or decision-making is required on the part of the youngsters. Less and less is required by parents in the way of family duties (such as house cleaning and yard work) which at one time were allocated to children. These trends are taking place within the middle-class life style. Nevertheless, as members of the working class (blue collar group) increasingly adopt the middle class as their reference group, they, too, are giving more to and requiring less of the younger family members.

Certainly cultural change cannot be designated as the only, or even the primary, etiological factor in the creation of dependency in the individual. Many individuals develop a high degree of independence within their personality structure in spite of dependency-producing tendencies within the culture. This fact, however, does not preclude the role of culture as one of the crucial factors in the dependency-producing process.

Social scientists have indicated a number of culturally produced processes which they cite as syntonic to the creation of dependency. Merton (1957) in his theory of "Social Structure and Anomie" described two types of dependent behavior whose causes he ascribed to the discrepancy which exists between the value structure which places a premium on material success and the true opportunity structure which does not provide similar access for all individuals to the means of attaining such success. Merton postulated that individuals adapt differently to this discrepancy. Two adaptive responses which are dependent in character are that of the "retreatist" who renounces all competitive goal-directed behavior which is normatively controlled and the "ritualist" who drowns his independent strivings in task conformity.

David Reisman's (1950) conceptualization of inner- and other-directedness is a theoretical formulation which, if accepted, targets cultural determinism as a pivotal variable in the causal sequence of dependency. If, as Reisman indicated, the precession of economic currents is such that the individual is becoming less related to material productivity (inner-directed) and more related to the provision and utilization of services with the attendant psychosocial transactions involved (other-directed), he is becoming increasingly interdependent. The interdependence required for the sustenance of the psychic economy implies a greater amount of dependency on the part of all members of society.

Levinson et al (1962) stressed the idea that culture in the United States has greatly increased the interdependent functioning of the individual and has served to increase dependency. He pointed out that the individual as a child, and later as an adolescent, is compelled to depend upon adults. As he moves toward adulthood, he makes a gradual transition from dependence to interdependence.

He is able to obtain satisfaction from dependence on others, provided that he, in turn, is able to allow others to depend upon him. In the work situation or within the company the individual depends upon the supervisor or his superior for guidance, direction, job security, etc. There are those who take the position that large corporations and "big government" involvement in the purveying of services are fostering dependency in the individual and robbing him of independent initiative by emphasizing and rewarding conformity and by creating the need for "belongingness" as described by W.H. Whyte (1957) in the well-known *Organization Man.*

Implications for Rehabilitation

Dependency can vary greatly from one individual to the next. The rehabilitation practitioner would be better able to develop an approach to the individual client by first ascertaining the type of dependency the particular client manifests.

Psychoanalytic Theory

Erikson's formulation as it applies to dependency has particularly important implications for the field of rehabilitation. Since the handicapped individual being rehabilitated is in a partially regressed state, his emotional responses may be, at times, childlike in character.

Utilizing Erikson's stages one can conceptualize the process of counseling in an Eriksonian framework. The patient places a "basic trust" in the rehabilitation professional who is helping him. If the counselor or the rehabilitation professional reciprocates this trust, especially his trust in the patient's efforts and ability to succeed, the patient's feelings of adequacy will be reinforced. He will then be motivated to try harder, participate more meaningfully in the rehabilitation plan, and be more willing to relinquish dependent behavior.

In similar vein, Erikson's concept of autonomy also has implications for the rehabilitation process. If the client is to move forward toward increased autonomous functioning, the counselor or other rehabilitation professional must concentrate on building up his feelings of adequacy. Conversely, the client's feelings of adequacy are built upon as the professional allows, encourages, and motivates the client to proceed more autonomously in his own rehabilitation.

The building of an identity is of crucial importance in the rehabilitation process if client dependency is to be reduced. In many cases the impact of a handicap, with its attendant feelings of difference, inadequacy, vulnerability, and defectiveness destroys or seriously impairs the client's identity. In a sense, the professionals involved in rehabilitation are confronted with the task of rebuilding an identity for the client. Almost all components which compose the handicapped client's identity change with the advent of handicap. Body image, vocation, mode of communication and social negotiation, and in some cases manner of locomotion become new and different. The synthesis of these components into a new and acceptable identity for the client is a difficult task. The counselor must be sufficiently sensitive to these identity needs and actively help the handicapped person in his struggle to understand and accept his modified identity. Frequently, helping the handicapped person to rebuild his identity involves the use of a role model.

Learning Theory

The reduction of dependency through the use of effective schedules and types of reinforcement would be of particular importance to practitioners in the field of vocational rehabilitation, specifically in rehabilitation counseling. It is well known that the disabled client regresses to a highly dependent state. What criteria does the counselor utilize to determine the technique of management of this dependency? Does he concentrate on providing a nurturing relationship for his client or does he use reinforcement techniques to obtain independent functioning? If the client's dependency level is not unusually high, a frequently used technique is to begin with a nurturing relationship and gradually nudge the client into increasing amounts of independent goal-directed behavior. However, there are many clients (such as disabled clients or those on public assistance) whose pattern of dependency is difficult to interrupt by this method. With such clients more definitive knowledge of the development of dependent functioning is required.

If dependency can be considered a learned response subject to positive and negative reinforcement, then the development of a schedule of positive and negative incentives could be developed as part of the rehabilitation counseling process. For the most part, present counseling techniques depend on the goal of vocational rehabilitation alone to motivate the client and counter his over-dependent strivings. This, in essence, demands that the client operate on the reality rather than the pleasure principle; in other words, forego the gratification of current dependent needs for the greater gratification of the more meaningful life which will follow successful rehabilitation. It may well be that interim rewards for successful achievement could be built into the counseling process. In this situation the counselor would be perceived as a parent-like authority figure.

The use of operant conditioning techniques should also be experimented with within sheltered workshops as well as in other training situations. Positive reinforcement is not infrequently utilized; however, negative reinforcement has rarely been attempted. If over-dependency is acquired as a learned response, it can be extinguished or at least partially extinguished during the rehabilitation process.

Developmental Theory

In adolescence interdependence becomes a crucial factor due to the importance of peer group acceptance. In rehabilitating adolescent clients, group techniques which utilize peer group identification may provide the transition from parental dependence to independence. Moreover, the involvement of parents in the rehabilitation of adolescents can be of definite value. If the parents cannot allow the healthy emancipation of the adolescent rehabilitee, the independent strivings of the client may be blocked and dependency reinforced. Counseling with the parents of adolescents becomes an important part of the rehabilitation process. In some instances parents feel a loss of control and are threatened by and rivalrous with the adolescent client. In these cases the provision of a relationship with a counselor, if not his child's counselor, is reassuring for the parent.

Sociocultural Theory

The implications of cultural factors must also be considered in the production or reduction of dependency in the rehabilitation process. Attempts by the practitioner to suggest a rehabilitation plan which involves goals and activities that run counter to the norms and values prevalent within the client's culture will be met by resistance which may take the form of a passive-aggressive expression of dependency. For example, if the client is part of an ethnic culture which places a premium on white collar work he may resent manual work to the point of resistance through dependency. The culture of the rehabilitation practitioner himself may influence the client's dependency or lack of it. If he comes from a culture which is caretaking and overprotective, he may overprotect and create dependency in his client. On the other hand, if the counselor is influenced by cultural factors which place a high value on autonomy, he may force a client into an independent role before he is actually ready for it. Also, if the client feels that he is unable to meet the demands for achievement inherent in our own American culture, he may just give up and lapse into dependency. Thus, reassurance of the client concerning his acceptance by the culture and, indeed, the creation of an accepting cultural milieu around the client during the rehabilitation process is of paramount importance.

Nevertheless, there are also those who do not view with alarm the dependent component of increasing interdependence. They hold that increasing interdependence is merely a fact of life that naturally accompanies the evolution of modern society with its population pressures and its rapid technological advance. It is the position of this group that technological and concomitant social change should evoke adaptive adjustment within an accelerating, dependent society rather than evoking anxiety and resistance.

If it is assumed that a certain amount of dependency is appropriate and, indeed, essential to the normal nurturance and development of the individual, one is faced with the problem of determining the point at which dependency becomes an impediment rather than being a part of healthy ego development. This critical dependency level undoubtedly varies among individuals. It is related to their level of psychodynamic development as well as to the situational pressures to which they are exposed. The functional and dysfunctional effects of dependency upon personality also depend upon the ability of the individual to recognize and accept his dependent strivings. Rehabilitation workers have long known that many of their clients have associated dependency with weakness and loss of control of the ego functions. Blocks to treatment in working with this kind of client are formidable, and a major part of the workers' therapeutic efforts must be initially directed toward the goal of helping the client accept his own dependent need without developing strong feelings of inadequacy.

Because of conflict over their own dependent feelings, many individuals deny their internal needs and react externally with what appears to be independent behavior. Not infrequently, the rehabilitation counselor is confronted with the client who denies his dependency, adopts an unrealistic perception of his handicap, and sets vocational goals that are unobtainable within his capacity.

It is important to recognize that dependency must be considered within the context of the social system within which it occurs. The rehabilitation of a handicapped individual takes place within a number of interacting systems. Each social system composed of a number of articulating roles influences the client's dependency needs and manifestations in a different way. The dependent responses of the client in a sheltered workshop will be quite different from those he will exhibit in a regular community work situation. Such differences must be understood and anticipated.

In conclusion, the behavioral scientist's problems with the nature of dependency might be likened to the physical scientist's problems with the nature of light. In neither case does the practitioner at this point, know quite what it is with which he is dealing. Yet, his tasks require that he describe, measure, and make work for him the forces and transactions related to concepts which he does not fully understand. What is most interesting is that he is frequently successful.

2 Behavioral Manifestations of Dependency

Behavioral Manifestations

Are there different types of dependency? If there appear to be different types, are they merely differing expressions or manifestations of the same basic attribute? Research and clinical observations have as yet provided no definite answers. Nevertheless, for the present it may be helpful to set down a typology of dependent behavior and to delineate such knowledge as is available about each type. Dependency can be classified into two major types according to Heathers (1955). He made a distinction between instrumental dependency, characterized by needs for help, and emotional dependency characterized by needs for reassurance, affection, or approval.

In this book dependency is classified in a pragmatic system, that is, in a manner that is most useful to those whose role it is to cope with it. For example, if a rehabilitation counselor understands the manifest differences between that dependency which occurs in the rehabilitation center and that which is seen in the welfare client who lives in the community, he is better equipped to plan a successful counseling strategy. Here, a social systems approach to the understanding of dependence can be helpful. The motivations as well as stresses and pressures that a patient sustains in contact with the organizational system of an institution in which he resides differ from those to which he is exposed as a member of his family system. The outer manifestations of dependent behavior change as the client's role changes and as the roles of those about him change. In short, the nature of the psychosocial transactions in which the rehabilitation client is compelled to participate influences his dependence.

Thus, by classifying dependency relative to the major type of environmental stimulus in the particular setting which triggers it off, one is at least able to think in terms of manipulating the environment in a therapeutic way as well as utilizing the counseling process to clarify excessive dependent needs for the client within a given social system. The rational suggested, then, is that manifest dependency can be classified within the following five categories:

1. Social
2. Emotional
3. Financial
4. Institutional
5. Psychomedical

15

Social Dependency

The socially dependent individual constantly requires help from people around him to negotiate in interpersonal relationships for the achievement of purpose-oriented behaviors involved in daily living. For example, there are those individuals who must have some intermediary to make appointments for them or to initiate the first contact for services which they require. In its extreme form this type of dependency is manifested in the multi-problem or hard-core family members who would literally die rather than go to a clinic, doctor, or hospital for medical treatment. Yet, if a social worker takes them by the hand, leads them to the clinic, stays with them, and negotiates with medical personnel for them, they are willing to accept medical attention. At this point the reader may attribute this behavior to cultural deprivation and the individual's fears and anxieties because of his lack of familiarity with medical care and procedures. While it is true that such fears and anxieties are present, the reluctance to secure medical attention in many such individuals does not diminish with increased familiarity but continues at the same level. As a result, their medical needs are met only by means of the intervention of a third party to negotiate for them in interpersonal transactions with authority (medical) figures.

Such social dependence may take place as a result of feelings of strangeness, alienation on the client's part, and a fear of coping with the unknown. On the other hand, it may result from a resentment and fear of authority. To the socially dependent individual any role cloaked in authority or related to an authority-based setting is regarded as a potential threat. Social workers and health and education personnel are looked upon with the same mistrust as are police. Yet, they require the help of these very professionals whom they mistrust. In a sense, the social dependent engages in a type of retreat from society. To him the demands of the society become overwhelming and his method of coping with these demands is to constantly seek interventive assistance of others.

Many handicapped individuals become socially dependent because of their feelings of difference from other members of society as well as their feelings of inadequacy relative to the existing norms of competition. In this respect physically, mentally, and socially handicapped individuals develop their own systems of norms and values. They function as a minority group. The sub-cultures of the deaf, the blind, and other groups have been noted (Wright, 1960). Although these individuals retreat from society into their own subcultures, they often seek the interventive help of non-handicapped society in meeting their needs.

The socially dependent may or may not be financially dependent. Social dependence exists among minority ethnic groups in their first years of residence in the United States. Psychologically, these individuals may be highly depended upon by others. Moreover, they may work and be financially independent. Yet, for an initial period while they are still alienated from the new culture in which they find themselves, they exhibit social dependence. That is, they constantly seek the intervention of others in their relationships with the social institutions.

Emotional Dependency

Emotional dependency is somewhat different in character from social dependency in that its goal is the direct satisfaction of deep emotional needs within the personality structure of the individual. It frequently occurs among family members. Its etiology can best be traced through the understanding of psychodynamic processes. There may be a high emotional component in social dependency and, indeed, in all the five categories stipulated. However, it must be remembered that the classification of dependency being proposed here is based not on basic origin or etiology but rather on locus and type of manifestation. In other words, there are some manifestations of each type of dependency in all types.

Emotional dependency is often characterized by a constant and inappropriate need for emotional support by one family or group member from another. At times this type of dependency takes the form of a need for generalized diffuse emotional support which the emotionally dependent person requires to continue functioning in a relatively adequate way. To illustrate, a wife who needs excessive expressions of love and approval from her husband exemplifies the emotionally dependent adult. Another example of such dependency is the child who hangs on his mother's apron strings.

Emotional dependency as it exists within the family constellation is usually one of neurotic origin. In some cases it is prompted by the existence of motives to satisfy unfulfilled needs for affection and nurturance. In other cases it is an expression of unconscious and sometimes conscious hostility against the person who is the target for dependent demands. In other words, the person who fills the needs of the hostile-dependent individual is virtually tied to him and kept in the state of an emotional slave.

Financial Dependency

Financial dependency is one of the most complex types of dependency both from the standpoint of comprehensibility and management. It is a problem which has been with us since the dawn of recorded history and promises to continue. The fight against dependency is no simple action but rather a major war. With over 25 million chronically ill and an estimated 3 million more eligible for vocational rehabilitation the magnitude of the task becomes apparent. Moreover, an estimated additional 35,000 individuals become eligible for vocational rehabilitation each year. Over 50 million people in the United States suffer poverty and some form of dependency. An aging population which includes approximately 19 million people half of whom suffer from poverty compounds the dependency problem and increases the need for rehabilitation services of all types. Considering that 12 million individuals in the United States are on public assistance, a substantial number of whom are physically and mentally disabled, the need for providing opportunities for rehabilitation becomes evident.

Several theories of causation have been proposed for this type of dependency. There are certain psychosocial theorists who maintain that financial dependence is a learned behavior and, in a sense, an operant response to positive reinforcement by the community which rewards dependency in the form of free income maintenance. The psychoanalytically-oriented theorists postulate a kind of sustained state of depression which these dependents suffer, stemming from both material deprivation and lack of love by parents during early childhood. This early deprivation of nurturance results in a type of emotional inertia which prevents independent behavior and results in a perpetual quest for love and nurturance throughout the life of the individual.

Partial confirmation of this theory was obtained by Goldin (unpublished paper) in a study of the Boston Chronic Family Project. It was noted that, frequently, highly financially dependent individuals would attempt a psychosocial role reversal in relation to their children. Parents who were suffering from the deprivational depression mentioned above would attempt to force their teenage children into independent roles; the former became increasingly dependent upon their children to make decisions and carry out important family activities, particularly those activities which relate to dealing with community institutions. The cultural component of financial dependency may be high. In other words, the financially dependent client may learn his dependent way of life, a life style quite different from that sanctioned by middle-class norms and values.

This type of dependency appears to be caused by a number of factors acting in combination. In some cases it has basis in reality, that is, gaps in the opportunity structure of the individual which prevent his independent functioning (lack of education, job opportunities, etc.). However, in many cases, even when the opportunity structure is modified in favor of the financially dependent client, he is resistive to moving in the direction of independence. Spencer (1970) showed that the structure and organizational dynamics of the helping agency influences the dependent behavior of its clients.

In focusing on the welfare client Pruitt and Van der Castle (1962) found that the chronically unemployed scored significantly higher on the Navran Dependency Scale than did the non-chronically unemployed. The chronically unemployed tended to give shading responses to Rorschach cards which contained a lesser degree of form quality, indicating more intense anxiety, feelings of inadequacy, etc., than did the non-chronic group as well as greater dependency imagery according to DeVos' scoring system. In this study chronicity was determined by case worker and supervisor ratings as the amount of public assistance received during the past year.

Levinson (1964) attempted to set up a system whereby the chronically dependent client could be classified in terms of his response to the social agency. Traditionally, a person was classified as chronically dependent if he was receiving help from one or more welfare agencies over a long period of time. However, because social workers employ basically the same treatment method for all clients, and all clients are not helped, Levinson suggested the separation of the chronically dependent group into three subgroups: moral, calculative, and alienative. The moral group would consist of those individuals who respond willingly to the agency's attempts to help because they share a common value system. The calculative group would consist of those individuals who respond only if there is material reward offered, no matter what the value system. The alienative group, the most difficult group to reach, would consist of those who do not respond to the agency's attempt to help because they do not share the same value system as that of the agency or of society at large. Levinson advocated a different treatment approach for each of these groups.

During the past ten years increasing attention has been given to the rehabilitation of chronic dependents with physical and mental handicaps. In general, success has not been striking, but what has taken place has been encouraging. The Social and Rehabilitation Service has initiated and sponsored a number of special demonstration and research projects in cooperation with welfare departments to test and study new methods and techniques of rehabilitating handicapped clients who are financially dependent and on public assistance. In addition, the Rehabilitation Service Administration has also been studying the application of concerted services in the fields of health, education, and welfare for the rehabilitation of financially dependent individuals living in low-cost housing projects (Spencer, 1966).

The high degree of complexity of the problem has been well documented by Cubelli (1962). His studies indicate that financial dependency rarely, if ever, appears in pure form but is usually compounded by several other types of pathology such as physical illness, mental illness, alcoholism, etc. His findings reveal a high incidence of family stress within financially dependent families with handicapped breadwinners. Whether the stress occurs as a result of the financial dependency or whether the financial dependency is a result of family stress is not known. However, Cubelli concluded from his data that while there are certain common psychological factors which are discernible in the financially dependent family, each family and, indeed, each individual must be approached on a highly diagnostic and individualized basis if they are to be helped. Goldin et al (1970) also maintain that whatever the individual situation, all financially dependent clients must be provided with a climate of enablement; that is, a nondefensive organizational climate which allows self determination for the client and affords him an improved opportunity structure within which to attain psychosocial growth.

Much is being learned concerning the rehabilitation of the financially dependent client. Rehabilitation professionals are learning that there must be a close relationship between attempts to modify the client's opportunity structure and his motivational structure. In the fight against dependency there has been a trend over the years to focus either on intrinsic or extrinsic motivational factors rather than to consider them equally important in motivating the disadvantaged. In the 1930's and 1940's, with the upsurge of psychoanalytic thinking, rehabilitation for the disadvantaged was seen to take place only if a modification in the psychodynamic structure of the individual could be accomplished. In the late 1950's and early 1960's the emphasis swung to changing the opportunity structure for the disadvantaged through re-education and job placement. Here it must be stated emphatically that the handicapped can be rehabilitated only if both the psychodynamic and opportunity structures are modified on an individual and diagnostic basis (Goldin et al, 1970). The individual who is intrapsychically blocked and unmotivated cannot make maximum use of an improved opportunity structure. On the other hand, even the most highly motivated and well balanced individual cannot raise himself from a position of disadvantagement if most paths of opportunity are closed to him. In other words, to make training and job opportunities available is not sufficient. Rather, it becomes necessary for rehabilitation counselors to regard the financially dependent client as a psychosocial-vocational entity, such that his social, emotional, and vocational needs will be met by a given vocational rehabilitation plan. This thesis is substantiated by a number of research reports compiled by Margolin and Goldin (1969).

Much research with multi-problem or hard-core dependent families has taken place over the last fifteen years (Buell, 1952; Wiltse, 1958; Cubelli, 1962; Furman, 1962; Ferman, 1969; Poussaint, 1969). A principal finding of this research is that in many of the families on public assistance the pattern of financial assistance is generational in character. In a significantly high number of cases these families have been on public assistance for two generations, three generations and in some cases even four generations.

As indicated earlier in this chapter, financial dependence from a psychological point of view is not necessarily a special kind of dependency. However, as a manifestation of dependency it has some unique characteristics which must be considered in the process of rehabilitation counseling with the handicapped client who is on some form of external income maintenance.

Institutional Dependency

The process of rehabilitation of the socially, mentally, or physically handicapped individual does not always begin in the general community. Frequently, such rehabilitation is initiated in institutions such as general hospitals, chronic disease hospitals, residential rehabilitation centers, mental hospitals, sanataria, institutions for the mentally retarded, and correctional institutions. Goffman (1964) termed these institutions "total institutions" and described them in terms of the following characteristics:

1. All aspects of life are conducted in the same place under the same single authority.
2. Each phase of the member patient's daily activity will be carried out in the company of a large batch of others all of whom are treated alike and required to do the same things together.
3. All phases of the day's activities are tightly scheduled, with one activity leading at a pre-arranged time into the next, the whole circle of activities being imposed from above through a system of explicit formal rulings and body of officials.
4. The contents of the various enforced activities are brought together as parts of a single over-all rational plan purportedly designed to fulfill the official aims of the institution.

Naturally, in some such total institutions individualization does take place and needs of patients are met on a diagnostic basis. However, in general the four characteristics are essentially true. In such an institutional climate there are negative forces which can create and foster intensification of dependency in the patient or inmate population. Basically, the patient is always aware that his essential needs for food, shelter, clothing, and medical attention will always be met, regardless of what he does or does not do. This situation creates a fertile environment for the growth and flourishing of dependency. Moreover there are not infrequent instances in which the patient's efforts to do things for himself are discouraged, blocked, or openly prohibited because they interfere with institutional routine, inconvenience staff, or require extra time that staff members find themselves unable to give. The very routinization of activities stultifies independent thinking; the patient who attempts to question the institution's way of doing things is regarded by staff not as an individual fighting dependence, but rather as a hindrance to the functioning of the institution. In addition to the dependency imposed by the social structure of the institution, the patient feels intrapsychically inadequate because he is always painfully aware that he is institutionalized because of some defect, unable to function adequately outside the institution's walls and deviant, even if temporarily so, from what is considered normative by society.

Paradoxically, then, the very social structure whose goal, in many cases, is to return the patient to independent functioning outside its walls creates a psychosocial milieu which is antithetical to this goal. This problem and its effects are documented by Margolin (1963) in his formulation of the "failure syndrome" in hospitalized mental patients. These patients suffer from an unconscious and, at times, conscious need to fail in their rehabilitation. Margolin pointed out that this failure seeking syndrome is set in motion by a threat to the patient's current feeling of security. In the hospital the patient has adjusted to a way of life that satisfactorily meets his needs for self-preservation. The patient may function well until some change has been instituted, such as movement from one ward to another or an impending discharge. In many cases, the prospect of discharge from the hospital threatens the mental patient's dependent status and represents a threat of such magnitude to his security that it stimulates failure-seeking activity. In speaking of the mental patient, Margolin (1955) summed up the problem of institutional dependency in this statement:

It is safer to suffer eternal bondage and mental invalidism because there is a certain amount of security within the confines of this towering isolation. In fact, failure becomes his only success. Thus, he learns a way of life which we may euphemistically call institutionalization or secondary gain from illness.

The primary means of combating institutional dependency lies in the philosophy, structure, and functioning of the institutional organization itself. The degree to which an institution is isolated from or linked to the ongoing activities of the community determines, to an important extent, the patient's motivation for independent functioning. Moreover, staff relationships and processes within the organization must be such as to stimulate independence rather than dependence in patients. Research has shown (Stanton and Schwartz, 1958) that staff attitudes and relationships appreciably affect the progress of the patient. For example, members of the nursing service, who help the handicapped patient get out of bed when the physical therapy department has recommended that the patient needs the exercise involved in getting out of bed himself, not only impede the physical rehabilitation of the patient but are instrumental in the reinforcement of dependency.

Because of the increasing proportion of hospitalized patients over age 65, self-care dependency among the elderly is becoming increasingly problematic for hospital personnel. Gurel and Davis (1967) surveyed the extent of self-care dependency among thousands of Veterans Administration Hospital patients. Using a self-care inventory, two nursing staff members in each of 11 hospitals rated patients (mean age, 67) on the extent to which they required physical assistance from others in accomplishing activities related to eating, dressing, bathing, eliminating, and moving about. Slightly better than one in ten patients were judged by one or both raters to be self-care dependent. To compound the problem, following-up ratings three and six months later indicated that over three quarters of the patients originally rated were still hospitalized. Gurel and Davis recommended that "except for unavoidable dependency in crippled or bed-ridden patients, it is more humanitarian and more economical to force patients into independence and to reinforce their attempts to achieve it."

The value of the therapeutic community as opposed to the custodial community has been well documented by Jones (1953), Greenblatt et al (1955), and Peffer (1956). A custodial type of environment fosters dependency and thwarts independent strivings. In the therapeutic community, on the other hand, all staff bend their efforts toward helping patients take independent steps. To fight dependency within the institutional setting a concerted effort is required by all staff members, not only by professional staff. To achieve this concerted effort the organizational processes of communication, coordination, and cooperation must be highly developed among the various disciplines and staff echelons. When the reduction of patient dependency becomes an organizational goal of the institution, success is possible.

Bergen and Thomas (1969) examined the widely accepted belief that the chronically ill *become* dependent upon a sheltered existence offered through hospitalization. Twenty acute, 20 2-year chronic, and 20 5-year chronic patients, all first admissions with schizophrenic or depressive psychosis and equally divided for sex, were interviewed regarding, among other things, their attitudes toward the benefits of hospitalization, the necessity of their hospitalization, their own mental illness, and their anxiety surrounding the return to community living. Interestingly, although both chronic patient groups expressed significantly greater anxiety about leaving the hospital setting than did the acute patient group, acute female patients expressed anxiety in proportions similar to chronic males and females. This suggests that males may develop institutional dependency over time while females may exhibit such dependency at the outset. One possibility offered was that acute males may have been able to maintain a tie between themselves and the community via their work, whereas acute female patients had already experienced isolation from the outside world through loss of emotional family ties. Other differences were nonsignificant. The authors suggested that prehospital experiences may be more critical in determining hospital dependency and identification than the socializing effects experienced during hospitalization.

Discharge of the patient from an institution can present problems both to the patient and to those concerned with his post-institutional adjustment. Wolkon (1968, 1970) described some of the characteristics of psychiatric patients who at hospital discharge expressed the need for and began and continued participation in a community based rehabilitation program. All patients were referred on the basis of need. Two thirds did not begin (attend at least twice) and of those who began, only one half continued (attended at least ten times). Among the patient variables related to beginning participation were marital status (single, divorced, separated, widowed) birth order (first-born or only child), current period of hospitalization (three months or more), patient perception that significant others in his milieu expected notable change in his task role performance, sources of income which included public monies, and "definitely yes" to a question regarding participation. Continued participation related only to first born status and patient expectation of little change in his level of social participation and task role performance. These relationships are interpreted in terms of dependency and affiliation needs as motivational factors influencing participation. The author warned that, if indeed community based rehabilitation outpatient facilities attract the more dependent client, there is danger that these services will become, like large state hospitals did, maintenance- rather than rehabilitation-oriented and perpetuate client dependency rather than foster interdependent and independent functioning.

Thus, in examining this study for its implication for rehabilitation we are reminded that the postinstitutional followup process is a two-edged sword. On the one hand, emotional support is a necessary component in the client's achievement of independence. However, dependence can also be fostered during this process. Hence, the rehabilitation worker must be constantly aware of the line which separates healthy support and destructive dependency producing behavior. The counselor or other rehabilitation practitioner must be able to differentiate true client cooperation from an overdependence on the treatment relationship.

Examples of ways in which problems of institutional dependency can be handled both within the facility and after discharge are illustrated, respectively, by the following two reports. Concerned about the negative effects of institutional life upon the functioning of mental retardates Miller and Paul (1970) related an incident involving mildly retarded young adult males whose bids for independence were met with encouragement rather than restraint. The training school atmosphere described both psychologically and in terms of physical planning, was geared toward diversity, variability, and flexibility and contributed greatly toward maintenance and development of skills necessary for attainment of the goal of successful functioning in the larger community. An organization designed specifically to help released patients adjust to the transition from hospital dependency to independent living in the community was reported by Cummings et al (1969). Established by a group of former hospital patients who underwent intensive milieu therapy while hospitalized, Mobilization for Maturity deals with and attempts to solve problems of daily living encountered by the disabled in the community through the principles embodied in milieu therapy. Community action, information and communications, and social and vocational readjustment programs were among the activities in which members were involved.

Psychomedical Dependency

A fifth manifestation of dependency may be called, for want of a better term, psychomedical. Psychomedical dependency refers to those dependent responses evoked by physical illness or handicap. This type of dependency is reality-based since the patient is, in fact, incapacitated and is compelled to depend on those around him to satisfy his reality needs. He is, in effect, placed in a position of childlike dependency and, in most cases, goes through a period of regression. However, the level to which the patient regresses and the length of time in which he remains regressed depend upon the nature of his dependent needs prior to the illness and attitudes of significant people in his psychosocial milieu. Psycho-medical dependency is a natural and symptomatic consequence of illness and should be accepted as part of the illness or handicap. However, the manner in which those who enter into social transactions with the patient deal with the dependency influences his recovery from the illness as well as his relationship to the rehabilitation process. Psychomedical dependency among emphysemics for example and its impact upon others was illustrated through case material presented by Scott (1969).

Heightened dependency needs often accompany periods of stress or anxiety, such as impending surgery. The effects of both dependency and anxiety on surgical recovery rate were investigated by Rothberg (1966). Eighty hospitalized males were given the Sixteen Personality Factor Questionnaire prior to and four days following hernia surgery in order to determine pre- and postoperative levels of anxiety and dependency. Recovery was measured in terms of rate of resumption of normal gastric, urinary, and bowel functioning and body temperature. It was hypothesized that men who tested comparatively high on dependency would also test comparatively high on anxiety and that both anxious and dependent men would recover more slowly than less anxious and dependent men. Results showed that neither dependence nor anxiety related to each other or to speed of recovery. Dependency was generally evident following surgery: initially dependent men scored essentially the same as they did presurgically while initially non-dependent men scored significantly higher postsurgically.

In a recent study of physical therapists Goldin (unpublished paper) found that respondents adopted one of three techniques in the management of dependency. One group adopted what might be termed a "reality-oriented" attitude toward dependency. This group, which comprised two-thirds of the sample, felt that it was important to motivate the patient to achieve his maximum potential within the limitations of his handicap. They felt that a certain amount of urging and pressure by those around the patient was acceptable as long as the patient was not pushed to try to achieve goals which were so difficult to attain that they aroused his anxiety.

A second group of therapists were governed in their motivation of patients by an "acceptance philosophy." They took the position that, although they were committed to the maximum rehabilitation of the patients, they could best meet their clients' psychological needs by not motivating them to fight actively the dependency of their handicap, but by helping to accept and live within the framework of limitations imposed by the disabling conditions.

The third group of therapists believed in approaching the dependency problems of the physically handicapped individual with what has been referred to as a "Spartan" philosophy. The approach is predicated on the idea that if rehabilitation expectations are set at a high level (in some cases higher than the patient's capacity warrants), he will strive to meet them if constantly urged and attain a higher level of rehabilitation than if goals set were completely within his capacity. The proponents of this point of view believe that the chronically ill and handicapped individual has far more potential for overcoming dependency and living a normal life than is ever tapped because he is incompletely motivated. This group is of the opinion that placing the patient under pressure to achieve and making demands are constructive devices. They are not concerned with the anxiety which the patient mobilizes over doubts of his success, nor do they feel that the patient's discouragement at failures along the way are detrimental to his personality functioning if adequate counselor support is provided. The professionals who are convinced of the efficacy of this approach in combating dependency in illness and handicap maintain that anxiety and frustration can be channeled constructively to become a positive motivating force. They point to such individuals as Helen Keller, Glenn Cunningham, Harold Russell, and Franklin D. Roosevelt as testimony to the validity of their hypothesis.

It is interesting to note that these physical therapists' approaches to dealing with dependency are also in the thoughts of professionals in the various disciplines involved in rehabilitation. A study by Goldin (unpublished paper) suggests that these same attitudes toward dependency in handicap and illness exist in the general population as well as in professionals in the field. No one of the three approaches is workable with all individuals in a state of psychomedical dependency. Among the factors to be considered in the treatment plan is the response of significant others to the handicapped individual and his disability.

While these three philosophical approaches relating to client dependency in the rehabilitation process may seem somewhat arbitrary, they do, nevertheless, provide a typology for understanding environmental response to handicaps which can be helpful to the practitioner.

In summary, an attempt has been made to classify or develop a typology of manifest dependency and to discuss some of its correlates. It is possible in a descriptive way to differentiate among its various manifestations. This course of action at least enables the rehabilitation clinician who must deal with dependency to identify dependent behavior in a manner which permits the development of coping techniques.

In setting down the typology the authors do not imply that expressions of dependency are caused by the external situations alone. It is recognized that intrapsychic dependency needs which have been built up within the personality structure of the individual throughout his life play an important part in determining the quality and intensity of the dependent response to situational factors discussed. While all five types of manifest dependency have been discussed under the head of "expressions" for the sake of convenience, they are not homogeneous in character. Financial, institutional, and psychomedical dependency may be brought about by given situations which are, in a sense, imposed by fate. Social and emotional dependency, on the other hand, tend to be more interpersonal and persist or transcend a number of situations.

It must again be emphasized that this classification of dependency expressions has as its purpose the analysis of responses as they occur within rehabilitation settings in order that the rehabilitation practitioner may take definite steps in the management of the client's dependency.

Implications for Rehabilitation

These, then, are five manifestations of dependency. There are other behavioral responses which cannot be classified as being essentially dependent but with which dependency has been found to be associated. The rehabilitation professional works with clients in various milieux. The hospital, the rehabilitation center, the sheltered workshop, and the community itself are all involved in the rehabilitation process. The dependence of the handicapped person is modified and molded by particular structures of the psychosocial situation in which the client finds himself at a given time. If the client is living with his family, the counselor must be prepared to deal with the neurotic type of emotional dependence which family relationships frequently evoke. If the client happens to be a long-term public assistance case, the counselor must be aware of and deal with the acquired life style of the confirmed financial dependent. Moreover, if the rehabilitation worker understands the client's alienation and the subsequent development of social dependence, he is in a good position to begin quickly the reintegration process which will decrease the client's feelings of resentment, mistrust, and fear of society so that he can rely on his own negotiative skills to get along.

Social Dependency

Sometimes the combating of dependency requires drastic measures. When the professional rehabilitation worker recognizes social dependency in a client, it may be necessary for him to literally "take the client by the hand" to involve him in the rehabilitation process. As rehabilitation progresses the rehabilitation worker should make attempts to wean the client away from his need for an intermediary to intercede for him in his relationships with authority and the community institutions. This is frequently a difficult task, since the client's resistance is usually great. However, as he achieves success in negotiating for his own needs, this resistance decreases. In other words, the rehabilitation worker must develop an approach which depends upon a combination of intervention in the client's behalf and nudging for independent forward movement. The professional helping person cannot compel the individual to relate to the social institutions. This course of action only raises his anxiety level and can result in his immobilization. It is rather a task of reeducation based on an operant rationale. The client is helped to experience a rewarding situation when he makes independent attempts at relating to community institutions and resources. This process is, of course, gradual and extended.

A major problem in dealing with the socially dependent client is the discouragement of the rehabilitation worker at the slow movement and apparent failure of the client to change. Yet, change can and does take place if the treatment relationship is strong enough. The socially dependent client is an individual who has been traumatized, not only by one person or a small group of people but by society in general. To achieve success with this type of client he must be integrated into a society of which he was never really a part.

Emotional Dependency

Emotional dependency in the family is of crucial importance to the practitioner in the field of vocational rehabilitation since significant members of the client's family are important in motivating him either positively or negatively. The McPhee studies (1963) clearly indicated that family support of the client in rehabilitation is of paramount importance in the success or failure of a rehabilitation plan.

The attitudes which family members adopt toward the client's dependent strivings can profoundly influence his motivation to work toward self-help in the rehabilitation process. For example, an overprotective wife or mother can raise the handicapped client's anxiety level to a point where he is fearful of attempting activities which are basic to his successful rehabilitation. On the other hand, if family members are unable to accept the usual dependent feelings commonly expressed by disabled people, they may adopt a "Spartan-like" attitude and push the client physically or emotionally into discouragement and consequent failure.

The reduction of emotional dependency poses complex problems for the practitioner in the field of rehabilitation because this dependency is conditioned by powerful relationships over which the professional has little direct control, namely, family relationships. The issue raised here is what is the rehabilitation worker's responsibility for counseling with families of their clients. There are those who would relegate this role to another agency (family counseling or psychiatric). On the other hand, some rehabilitation counselors work directly with family members to resolve overdependent relationships which are blocking their client's movement.

There are instances in which emotional dependency can be channelled constructively even if it cannot be fully reduced. For example, if a client has a particularly strong dependent relationship with a certain family member, the family member, if properly counseled, can make demands upon the client for some independent action in certain areas of functioning. The client, rather than lose the gratification of the emotional relationship, will with urging be willing to undertake certain independent action in behalf of his own rehabilitation.

In the final analysis a dependent relationship is at least dyadic and its nature and configuration are as much determined by the manner in which the target individual reacts to the dependent person's demands as it is by the psychology of the individual from whom the dependent behavior emanates. In this regard, suggestibility of the dependent individual and his conformity become key variables in the determination of the course of the dependent relationship.

Financial Dependency

With the financially dependent rehabilitation client a brand of intensive counseling is required in which the counselor uses his helping relationship to provide what may be called "focused emotional support." By this term it is meant that the counselor remains sensitive to particular segments or problem areas in the client's social and vocational functioning. He encourages him and, to some extent, directs his activities in these areas. In this respect the counselor allows a certain amount of dependency in the helping relationship while at the same time is actively pushing for independent reality testing and confrontation on the part of the financially dependent client. While counseling in this manner, the counselor must stay carefully attuned to the normative and value systems of the client's subculture and gear rehabilitation procedures to change the value structure of the client and indeed manipulate, if necessary, his cultural milieu by exposing him to a totally new environment. Only when such social resonance is attained can the counselor truly communicate with the financially dependent rehabilitation client. However, the achievement of a strong helping relationship with the financially dependent individual is difficult because of the intense emotional demands of the client. Goldin observed (unpublished paper) that not infrequently social workers and counselors actually take on a kind of situational depression as a result of prolonged work with this type of client. Not only does the financially dependent person lean heavily on the worker for support, but the emotional and professional gratification of the worker are minimal. With the highly financially dependent client much effort is required on the part of the counselor to achieve small amounts of positive movement. Yet, it is important to note that Craddock et al (1970) demonstrated that, when the client's expectations of himself and the counselor's expectations of the client could be changed from negative to positive, success ensued.

If we accept Levinson's classification of the chronically dependent group into the subcategories of moral, calculative, and alienative, the rehabilitation counselor or practitioner must orient himself differently to each of these sub-groups. The morally involved group might respond to a suggestive treatment technique which would involve invoking the norms and values of society which place a premium on independent functioning, self-support, and individual attainment. The calculative group might respond to treatment which relied on the positive reinforcement of tangibles and the self-gain of the individual client. The alienative group would pose a far more difficult problem for the individual in that treatment might have to be directed toward the reclamation of the client into the mainstream of society. This treatment technique would require that the client be convinced that the norms and values of society relative to rehabilitation were good and self-satisfying and that the rewards of society's approbation had meaning. Nevertheless, it must be recognized that the alienative client is one whose relationship to his social group may stem from psychopathology which must be dealt with on a deeper psychotherapeutic level. Such treatment may not be within the purview or capability of the rehabilitation practitioner.

Institutional Dependency

The rehabilitation professional who treats clients in an institutional setting can function more effectively in the management of client dependency if he realizes the profound effects of the institution's social structure upon the personality of his client. Although the worker cannot make major changes in the organization's social system, he can intervene in his client's behalf at key points and negotiate with the institution's personnel to allow and stimulate a measure of independent functioning in the client. If active volunteer programs are instituted and patients are allowed to participate in community activities, it becomes more feasible to integrate patients as part of the community when they are ready for discharge and vocational rehabilitation. Such an approach requires that the institution involve itself in community planning and organization so that it becomes a recognized part of the network of community agencies. It also means that professionals must accept constant interpretation of the institution's functions and purpose as a part of their professional role.

Psychomedical Dependency

With the use of the psychomedical classification one can see vast implications for the rehabilitation counselor. First, this typology can help to create a self-awareness in the rehabilitation profession relative to his own attitudes toward client dependency. The practitioner who is "Spartan" in the excessive demands he places upon his clients may create anxiety which can immobilize the client while it mobilizes increased dependent strivings. On the other hand, the professional who operates on a total acceptance philosophy runs the risk of overprotecting his handicapped clients and failing to motivate them to fight their own dependent strivings.

Secondly, it is most helpful if, in a general way, the counselor can classify his client's response to his own dependent strivings. This diagnostic stratagem holds implications in formulating a rehabilitation plan for the client. If a particular client has "Spartan" leanings in his personality, the counselor may be able to take advantage of these in working out a rehabilitation plan which is somewhat more difficult and makes great demands upon the client's capacities. Yet, to move a client who is highly dependent into a program which makes such "Spartan" demands constitutes poor rehabilitation planning and will frequently end in failure. The client who accepts his limitations realistically but is willing to work to his optimal capacity can be approached as one without these serious problems.

However, most professionals who work with the ill and handicapped would agree that, regardless of the personality structure of the patient, it is important for those around him to sympathize and accept his dependency. This does not imply that no attempts are to be made to motivate independent functioning in the patient. It does mean, however, that those around the patient convey that they accept the fact that the dependency is reality-based and make no attempt to deny or prevent the patient from expressing his dependent feelings. This point is stressed because there are individuals who are unable to accept their own dependent feelings. They cannot tolerate dependent feelings in others because they arouse their own dependency conflicts. The person with this type of personality structure frequently reacts to the dependent patient with hostility. At times this hostility is unconscious; at other times conscious and suppressed. Sometimes it is openly expressed. Nevertheless, whatever form this hostility takes, the patient usually perceives it and reacts adversely to it. Equally as problematic is the therapist or counselor who reacts to the patient's psycho-medical dependency with anxiety because it mobilizes fantasies concerning his own defectiveness and possible mutilation ("there but for the grace of God go I" and "it could happen to me"). Professionals who react to psycho-medical dependency in this manner should be helped to work through these feelings. Members of the patient's family who have these problems can be helped by counseling, medical casework, and psychiatry.

3 Dependency Research

The development of methodological procedures for the study of dependency involves difficult problems. Unlike a chemical or a microorganism, dependency cannot be isolated but of necessity must be studied as it occurs in combination with other personality traits or attributes. There is always the possibility that the responses of subjects are reflecting not only the trait of dependency but are being contaminated by other traits. If dependency is regarded organismically, it can be conceptualized as a trait. However, it can be considered also as a response variable.

Methodological Procedures

In attempting to identify dependency as a variable, four major methodological approaches have been utilized:

1. Psychological tests
2. Ratings and sociometric techniques
3. Laboratory behavioral measures
4. Biographical data

Although total reliance on psychometric tests in evaluating the rehabilitation client is frowned upon by some who maintain that they are poor substitutes for good interviewing skills, the judicious use of selected tests could be helpful. Laboratory behavioral measures are usually not available to the rehabilitation practitioner. However, biographical data can be obtained from most clients. The use of sociometric methods for identifying dependency, while not usually possible in the counseling setting, might be effectively attempted in group settings such as the sheltered workshop and rehabilitation center.

In developing a psychometric approach, psychologists hypothesize that certain normal personality variables are components of dependency and that these components are identifiable and measurable. Among the most commonly considered are submission, affiliation, need for nurturance, succorance, and deference. Although the Rorschach, Thematic Apperception Test (TAT), and other projective tests have been used to measure these variables, research for the most part has been with the pencil-and-paper tests. In some instances, special tests have been constructed; in other instances, scales derived from existing tests

33

such as the Minnesota Multi-phasic Personality Inventory (MMPI) and the Edwards Personal Preference Schedule (EPPS) have been utilized.

The MMPI consists of 550 statements which the subject is asked to sort into true, false and cannot say categories. Personality characteristics are assessed on the basis of nine clinical scales. In a study by Navran (1954), 16 judges chose those items on the MMPI which they considered to be indicative of dependency and specified the direction in which a dependent person would respond. Internal consistency was determined for two samples of 50 neuropsychiatric patients and cross validation procedures were carried out between the two sample populations. The final scale consisted of 57 of the original 157 items, the reliability for which was .91 for 100 patients.

Interestingly enough, because psychiatrists, psychologists, social workers, and counselors use the term freely, some practitioners treat dependency as though it were a validated psychological construct. To test the construct validity and meaningfulness of the concept of dependency, Nelson (1959) had psychotherapists administer to 80 patients a semantic differential and several direct measures of dependency, one of which was the MMPI, and then rate the extent of dependent behavior manifested by these patients in the therapy situation. Although ratings of behavioral dependency and dependent responses on the semantic differential were found to correlate positively, no relationship was established between scores on the Navran dependency scale and either dependency in psychotherapy or length of treatment. A high negative relationship was established between dependency and ego strength. It was concluded that dependency is conceptually meaningful but remains to be experimentally validated as a construct.

The EPPS provides measures of 15 personality variables through the use of a schedule that consists of pairs of statements from which the subject is told to choose that which is most characteristic of himself. Dependency has been defined as the score at or above the 70th percentile on deference and at or below the 50th percentile on autonomy with a minimum of 30 points between; independence, in the opposite direction (Bernardin and Jessor, 1957).

One Rorschach index to evaluate dependency involves a scoring system devised by DeVos (1952). In order to achieve a more quantitative system of scoring, DeVos had judges categorize affective content contained in Rorschach responses. Dependency, one of several categories, was further divided into eight subcategories based on Rorschach and psychoanalytic research. The new scoring system was then applied to 60 normal, 30 neurotic, and 30 schizophrenic protocols. Schizophrenics were found to differ from normals and neurotics, one large difference resulting from the subcategory, oral-fetal dependency.

DeVos' method for scoring affective content was simplified by Levitt, Lubin, and Zuckerman (1962). Using two groups of student nurses and two raters, reliabilities obtained for dependency were similar to those obtained by DeVos. The data were then validated on the Zuckerman Grosz (1958) sample of student nurses.

The TAT (as well as other projectives) has been used to tap dependency needs. The TAT is a method of revealing some of the dominant drives, emotions, sentiments, complexes, and conflicts of a personality through the use of a series of pictures about which the subject is encouraged to invent stories. The use of stories or story completion tests may be regarded as involving the same principles that apply to other fantasy productions of the TAT type. The only important difference lies with the stimuli employed (in one case, a title, in the other, a picture). That it is a most natural approach to the fantasy lives of children is evidenced by their story-telling behavior.

A more sophisticated approach to the study of dependency involves tapping both overt and covert manifestations of behavior. In a validity study, Werts (1961) administered to 40 primarily out-patient veterans the Rorschach, MMPI, and the Weschler-Bellevue and also obtained from each a vocational history. The protocols were ranked by judges for dependency, ego strength, intelligence, and social adjustment. Only the construct dependency was found to have cross-test validity.

A comparison of self report and projective methodologies was made by Zuckerman et al. (1961). Student nurse ratings of each other were likened to their self-ratings and scores on direct measures (Gough's Dominance Scale, Navran's Dependency Scale, EPPS) and indirect measures (Rhode Sentence Completion Test, Rorschach, TAT) of dependency. In general, direct measures of dependency related significantly better to peer ratings than did the less direct measures.

Another method for measuring dependency is that of direct observation. This technique has been used primarily for studying dependent behavior among children. The rater, either superior or peer, judges behavior according to rating scales consisting of certain personality or behavioral dimensions. The behavior being observed may occur within a structured experimental situation or within relatively unstructured common life surroundings such as the home or class-room.

There are several problems in the measurement of dependency. Chief among these is the occurrence of conflict over dependency. Because independent functioning is highly valued in our culture, some individuals cannot face their deeply seated dependency strivings and react with what outwardly appears to be independent behavior. Thus, if an experimenter is using the subject's request for help as an index of dependency, he may, for some individuals, actually be measuring the existence of conflict over dependency rather than the absence of the dependency drive. If conformity is utilized as an index of dependency, some subjects may well react to the rejection of their own dependency needs by non-conforming behavior. In an attempt to deal with this problem, Schwaab (1959) constructed a test designed to measure dependency conflict. He used a multi-choice story-completion technique with the purpose of identifying con-flicted and non-conflicted subjects. Subjects were then classified into one of the following three groups: 1) dependency acceptors, 2) dependency deniers, and 3) dependency vacillators.

While this instrument is a useful beginning in dealing with the problem of dependency conflict in that a method of measurement has been developed, it has as yet not been sufficiently standardized to evaluate accurately its validity and reliability. The perplexing aspect of dependency conflict is that, although one can postulate that it exists, there is no present way of knowing its prevalence. As a result, its importance is also a matter of some conjecture.

Nevertheless, the concept of dependency conflict has been receiving increasing attention. One of the prevailing theories of the etiology of alcoholism is based upon this concept. The alcoholic is theorized to be an individual with very strong needs for nurturance and affiliation. Unable to face or unaware of these needs, the alcoholic drinks himself into a state in which he is dependent upon those around him. However, since he perceives drinking as an independent, masculine endeavor, he is able to defend himself against the recognition of his dependent strivings.

Brudbard (1964) and Fitzgerald (1958) were two who experimentally approached the area of dependency conflict. Brudbard defined conflict as a low score on the Navran and predicted low scorers (dependency deniers) would perform similarly to high scorers (dependency acceptors) in a conformity situation. Partial confirmation was obtained.

Fitzgerald postulated that frequency of dependency responses obtained through projective techniques would correlate positively with overt dependency behavior and dependency conflict. Both dependency and conflict were defined in terms of Rotter's theoretical model of social learning which involves the concepts, need-value and freedom of movement. Conflict was said to result when need-value (the value the satisfaction of a given need has for an individual) is higher than freedom of movement (the expectation that the need can be met). Dependency was defined by the need to obtain need satisfaction through others. Frequency of dependent responses for the ISB, but not for the TAT, was found to be positively related to sociometric and interview data. The hypothesis that dependency conflict would be related to frequency of dependency on the TAT was supported. The use of sentence completion techniques in the identification of dependency in rehabilitation clients certainly merits further exploration.

The relation between self-report and projective methods was approached in a different manner by Braginski (1965). College students and V.A. general medical patients were compared for overt dependent behavior as reflected by both direct and indirect measures of dependency. Subjects were classified as congruent or non-congruent on the basis of test scores. Congruent subjects were those whose scores on the direct and indirect tests were consistent; non-congruent, those whose scores were discrepant. It was predicted that, in general, congruent test performance would manifest itself in behavior that was in agreement with the personal feelings of the individual rather than with the expectations of the larger social group. The prediction was not confirmed by behavioral observations of students in the classroom or by patients in hospital setting.

The following studies illustrate additional tests and methods that have been developed to measure dependency. Still others will be introduced in subsequent sections of this chapter. In order to measure personality variables in relatively pure forms, Comrey and Schlesinger (1962) constructed a scale of factored homogeneous item dimensions (FHDI). The questionnaire, consisting of 32 personality dimensions and four validity scales, was completed by 506 community and student volunteers. From a factor analysis of these variables and nine additional background data variables, shyness, dominance, hostility, compulsiveness, and dependency emerged as significant factors. Factors with substantial loadings on dependency were conformity (.66), need for approval (.61), and succorance (.61). While the dependency factor on this instrument remains to be validated, it has been identified and isolated.

On the basis of subsequent data obtained from a group of 252 college students, Jamison and Comrey (1968) redefined the dependence factor as "two quite different though somewhat overlapping" personality dimensions—dependence and socialization. Factors with loadings of .47 or better on dependence were conformity, need for approval, succorance, lack of self-sufficiency, and need for love. Factors with loadings of .47 or better on socialization were conformity, acceptance of social order, compliance, intolerance of nonconformity, respect for law, and welfare of loved ones.

Merenda et al. (1960) tested the extent to which the Activity Vector Analysis Test (AVA) is a measure of passive dependency and, as such, correlates with the Kessler Passive Dependency Scale (KPDS). Both tests were administered to male and female adults. Subjects were divided according to sex and classified as passive or nonpassive dependents on the basis of the KPDS. Mean AVA vector scores for each group were obtained. Comparisons indicated that passive dependents were less aggressive and less sociable, possessed a greater degree of emotional control and described themselves as more socially adaptable than the nonpassive dependents. Both scales yielded a higher passive dependency personality component among females.

Fordyce (1953) developed an instrument to measure dependency, the items of which involved descriptions of self and ideal self and recalled descriptions of parents. Items were classified as dependent-independent, behavior-feeling, and social desirability and were balanced throughout the scale. Male psychiatric patients were divided into high and low dependency groups on the basis of self-concept. Results indicated that groups could not be differentiated by their ideal self-descriptions, the discrepancy between self- and ideal self-descriptions, recalled descriptions of mother, or the degree of correspondence between self-description and recalled description of mother. Independent males, however, did describe their fathers as more independent and because of the correspondence between their self-concept and that of their fathers, they were said to identify with their fathers. Both groups leaned in the direction opposite to their classified independency-dependency status in describing their ideal selves.

A true-false test was developed by Golightly et al. (1970) to test dependency in children between eight and twelve years of age. For purposes of establishing reliability, nearly 200 middle to upper class white children at an urban parochial school were tested; overall test-retest reliability was .79. The data also provided some validation of the scale. Dependency scores were found to have decreased as a function of increasing grade level and girls, in general, tested more dependent than boys. Further, when compared to a group of lower class rural black children, the urban children tested significantly less dependent. Teachers' ratings of dependency among their pupils did not, however, correlate significantly with the scale scores. With additional research, the Children's Dependency Scale may prove to be a most valuable and efficient instrument with which to measure dependency in youngsters.

Cotler et al. (1970) developed and described in detail an operational measure of necessary and unnecessary goal-oriented, help-seeking dependency. Briefly, participants in a "quiz game," "contestant" (subject) and a "helper" (confederate who responds correctly and incorrectly to requests for help on a 50 percent schedule), write their answers to 40 general information questions. After rating his answers on a seven-point confidence scale, the subject may give the experimenter his tentative answer as his final answer or he may ask his "helper" for help before giving the experimenter his final answer. Responses and their rewards fall into the following four categories: (1) no help asked, tentative answer is final answer and incorrect, loss of two tokens; (2) no help asked, tentative answer is final answer and correct, gain of two tokens; (3) help asked, final answer (which may or may not be tentative answer) is incorrect, loss of one token; (4) help asked, final answer (which may or may not be tentative answer) is correct, gain of one token. Inappropriate or unnecessary help-seeking occurs when help is requested when the tentative answer is correct. As the authors pointed out, such a measure of dependency is more objective than observational measures, separates emotional and instrumental dependency, and can serve to supplement both observational and paper-and-pencil measurement techniques.

Dependency in the Non-Handicapped

Dependency manifests itself in the non-handicapped individual as well as in the severely ill and handicapped. Research in this area has yielded valuable insights into the psychological and developmental bases of dependency in general and suggests potential clinical applications.

Sex Differences and Sex-Role Identification

Dependent behavior exhibited in childhood and in adulthood may be partially determined by the sex role model of the child. The differential development of independence in infant monkeys as a function of their sex was investigated by Jenson et al. (1968). Five male and five female monkeys were observed in interaction with their mothers during the first 15 weeks of life. The results indicated that mothers played an active role in encouraging an earlier and greater mutual independence between themselves and their sons by more frequent punishment behavior and less frequent behaviors involving other forms of physical contact. Suggested factors to account for the differential maternal responses included biological differences in infant monkeys and their mothers and previous social learning experiences of the mothers.

Hartup and Keller (1960) studied dependency and nurturance behavior as a function of age and sex in preschool children. Measures of dependency and nurturance were obtained through teacher ratings of classroom conduct. Neither the age nor the sex variable correlated with behavior. Significant positive relationships were established between nurturance and help-seeking and physical affection-seeking dependency behaviors; negatively related to nurturance was the dependency of being near.

In order to test the assumption that dependence is related to identification with a female role model and independence with a male role model, Lansky and McKay (1969) instructed teachers to rate 20 male and 16 female kindergarteners on dependence-independence using the Beller scales and administered to the children the It Scale for Children and the Drawing Completion Test to assess manifest and latent masculinity-femininity, respectively. Boys did not differ from girls on dependency while, contrary to expectations, girls were rated higher than boys on independence. Although boys showed a greater preference for the masculine role on an overt level, they did not differ from girls for latent masculinity-femininity. Overt sex role preference was unrelated to dependency for both sexes. For boys, latent masculine sex-role identification was related to low dependence but, for girls, to higher dependence. The latter finding suggests that in girls dependence of an active nature (e.g. seeking help, seeking attention, seeking recognition, etc.) may be symptomatic of unconscious conflict over sex-role identification. Thus, at the kindergarten level, a simple relationship between dependence-independence and masculinity-femininity is questionable.

To test the hypothesis that sex role identification is a function of the dependency relationship the child enjoys with his parents and the extent to which his parents are able to meet his needs for dependence, Doherty (1969) administered to 736 college females the EPPS (n succorance), Leary's Inter-personal Check List (similarity of child-parent description), and Schaefer's Parental Behavior Inventory (parental nurturance and control). Women who described themselves as similar to their mother in turn described their mother as the more accepting parent; women who described themselves as similar to their father described their mother as controlling and expressed feelings of dependence on their father. These and other results suggested that sex role development is not simply a function of parental identification.

A more inclusive approach to the study of dependency in children considers dependency in parents and parental expectations for independence achievement.

Lederman (1964) administered to parents of nursery school children the EPPS for a measure of dependency and the Winterbottom Standards of Independence and Mastery for a measure of expectations for independence in their children. The Beller Scales were used to rate the children for dependency in the classroom situation. The hypothesis that level of dependency would be most alike between mother and daughter and between father and son was not supported.

Based upon Lynn's theoretical framework (see p. 75) Sherman and Smith (1967) predicted that orphans would be less cue dependent than children from normal family situations. Their prediction was generated from the presumed differences in the sex-role identification process for boys and for girls: because of the relatively high availability of the mother figure in the home, females are able to identify with their mother by direct imitation, while boys learn to identify by abstraction or by imitation of the masculine role model in lieu of a father who is absent from the home a great deal while working. It follows, then, that orphans who are raised by many adult caretakers would rely less upon specific characteristics of any one caretaker but, rather, identify abstractly with a composite role model based upon many. Thus, as males generally test less cue dependent than females, so orphans would be expected to exhibit less cue dependence than children from normal families. Parochial school children (mean age 13) served as subjects. Results of performance on a concept learning task showed that normal females were significantly more cue dependent than normal males and that orphan females were significantly less cue dependent than normal females. Contrary to expectations were the findings that orphan males were more cue dependent than normal males and more cue dependent than orphan females. In light of the fact that orphan girls were cared for by nuns (less imitable) and orphan boys by full-time male student counselors (more imitable), the authors interpreted the findings as supportive.

Parents who allow their child to participate actively in his environment might be expected to possess a relatively high degree of psychological differentiation and to encourage "interdependence" in their child, while parents who view their child during his developmental years as a passive recipient of their goals and wishes might be expected to be relatively undifferentiated and to encourage in him a "unilateral" orientation to the world. In order to assess parent-child conceptual structure, Cross (1970) administered the Hunt sentence completion test to sixth grade boys and girls and interviewed their parents regarding their approach to child rearing (discipline, etc.). Mothers of daughters who had attained a more differentiated conceptual structure were significantly more likely to have provided their child with an interdependent environment in which to grow than mothers of daughers low on conceptual structure. Mother-son, father-son, and father-daughter relationships were not significant. The results were discussed in terms of the differential influence that mothers and fathers as role models have upon their sons and daughters through preadolescence.

During the course of development, most children learn to identify with the parent of the same sex when both parents are available for imitation. DuHamel & Biller (1969) introduced to the traditionally conceived two-choice parental imitative preference situation an alternative choice, the opportunity to identify with neither parent. This was done in order to test the hypothesis that boys, having been reinforced to a greater extent than girls for independent action, would be more likely than girls to choose, if available, a nonparent object with which to identify. Each of 32 boys and 31 girls of kindergarten age were asked to move a child doll representing himself to one of three non-sex-typed figures (experimenter-designated mother, father, and nonidentified figures) in response to questions such as "Which of these three people is nice?" When the descriptive words used were within the child's vocabulary, the hypothesis was confirmed. It was suggested that imitative behavior may be related to dependence, nonimitation to independence. If these findings hold for adults then the rehabilitation counselor, through fostering identification, can use himself as a role model with dependent clients so that work habits and motivation for a higher level of functioning can be acquired through imitative behavior.

Early Parental and Developmental Factors

Moore (1965) investigated the effect of child rearing practices on the autonomy and dependency behavior of nursery school children. The subjects were families taking part in the Purdue Longitudinal Study and included 29 boys, 24 girls, and their parents. Child rearing practices were assessed by rating scales based on interview material from parents. On two occasions, 4 months apart, nursery school teachers rated the children on various aspects of behavior, including dependency and autonomy. Several relationships between child rearing practices and autonomy-dependence behavior in the children were found. Dependency in boys related to the use of physical punishment by mothers; dependency in girls, to severe maternal demands for mature behavior. Autonomy, on the other hand, appeared to have stemmed from available but nondemanding fathers for boys; for girls, from maternal permissiveness or from maternal rejection coupled with high paternal interest.

Clapp (1967) studied the effects of parental treatment on the development of dependence and competence in four-year-old boys. The sample consisted of 34 nursery school boys who, after a six-month observation period, were judged as most clearly representing competent and dependent children. On the basis of observed parent-child interaction, parent-completed paper-and-pencil tests, and family interview material, it was shown that parents of children judged competent (vs. dependent) were more likely to have treated their children as children (appropriate dependency need satisfaction) rather than as adults (inappropriate demands for independence). Treatment of their children as babies (inappropriate dependency need satisfaction) did not distinguish parents of competent from parents of dependent children. Further, parents of competent children were viewed as less restrictive, warmer, more competent themselves, and more consistent than were parents of dependent children.

Parents who meet their child's needs for dependence will, according to role theory, serve as models from which their child can learn, in turn, to be nurturant toward others. Eininger and Hill (1969) predicted that children who are instrumentally or emotionally dependent upon others will behave toward others in a reciprocal manner. Nursery school teachers divided 32 female preschoolers into affection seekers (person-oriented or emotionally dependent) and help seekers (task-oriented or instrumentally dependent), whichever need appeared to dominate. Each child was observed for six minutes in a doll play situation and their responses to prerecorded dependency statements originating from within the doll were recorded. Affection seekers reciprocated with significantly more affection responses than did help seekers; help seekers did not reciprocate with more help-giving responses than attention seekers, although differences were in the direction predicted. The latter finding was interpreted in terms of the relative situational nature of help-giving as opposed to affection-giving.

The presence and/or accessibility of the mother, especially during childhood, may be another factor which contributes to dependency. In a study by Waldrop and Bell (1963) dependency was operationally defined by the frequency with which teacher contact was initiated by preschool boys. It was postulated that frequency of teacher contact is related to family size and density. As predicted, children from large high density families sought out the teacher more than children from smaller less dense families. Lack of maternal availability in the home was proposed to account for the results.

In a later study Waldrop and Bell (1966) postulated that in addition to lower maternal availability, congenital factors would play a role in the subsequent dependency behavior of infants born to large high density families. Prior to their regularly scheduled feeding, 74 newborns (mean age, 80 hours) were observed in the hospital nursery and indices of activity were obtained (e.g. non-nutritive sucking, crying). Two and one half years later these boys and girls were observed in a school nursery. As expected, children who were lethargic as infants came from large high density families and exhibited greater dependency in the classroom in terms of seeking teacher contact.

Scodel (1957) compared frequency of dependency imagery on the TAT with breast size preference among males. Results indicated that subjects producing the greater number of dependency themes chose small-breasted women. Psycho-analytically oriented theorists would have predicted opposite results on the basis that lack of early reinforcement, resulting in the repression of dependency needs, would lead to symbolic gratification of those frustrated needs in later life through large breast preference. Scodel, on the other hand, posited that the less the reinforcement in early life, the less satisfaction, and the less the large breast would be sought. The primary difference between these two interpretations appears to lie with the relative importance accorded to need frustration and need satisfaction.

Mother attitude has been shown to be a factor in the development of dependent behavior in the child. McAlister (1965) investigated the effect of birth order on mother behavior toward her child. Twenty-one only children, 20 first-borns, and 20 later-borns were each observed in two mother-child situations. In one instance the child evoked the mother's pleasure; in the other, displeasure of the mother was created by the child's activity. Mothers of first-born and only children were rated as tending to be more interfering, incongruous, and excessive in their attitudes toward them. In addition, these children exhibited greater dependency than later-borns. However, research done by Harrison (1964) was not supportive of these findings.

The effect of father absence on the personality development and adjustment in children has been the subject of several investigations. The following two studies are illustrative (see also Wohlford and Liberman, p. 74). Dependency was one of several variables studied but only those results pertaining to dependency will be presented here. Santrock (1970) observed the dependency behavior of 30 male and 30 female lower class black preschoolers in a doll play situation and interviewed their mothers regarding the child's independence-dependence, the child-parent relationship, the presence or absence of a father substitute, other children in the family, and the like. For half of the children, fathers were absent due to divorce, separation, or desertion for a minimum of two years prior to the study; for the remainder, fathers had been absent from the home for no more than a total of one month. Results showed that father-absent boys were significantly more dependent than father-present boys on the basis of both doll play and maternal interviews; father-absent and father-present girls did not differ for dependency. On the basis of maternal interviews only, father-absent boys with no father substitute and father-absent girls with older female siblings only (vs. older male siblings only) were significantly more dependent than their father-absent counterparts. The effect of cause of father absence as well as onset of absence was investigated by Santrock and Wohlford (1970). The responses of 30 father-absent and 15 father-present lower class white male fifth graders to six free-response doll play situations designed to provide an index of dependency were obtained. Neither age at loss (0–2 vs. 3–5 vs. 6–9) nor reason for loss (death vs. separation, divorce, desertion) was found to relate significantly with dependency.

Behavior such as making extraordinary requests and demands of psychiatrists, nurses, and other key figures for time, attention, and services was defined as dependent in a study by Barry et al. (1965). A sample of 15 adult psychiatric patients whose mothers had died when the patients were aged three months to four years were compared with a matched group whose mothers had died when the patients were aged 11 to 17 years. Dependency was found to be a prominent characteristic of 13 of the early bereaved patients while only four of the 15 later bereaved patients exhibited such behavior.

By studying dependency in subjects over time, each serves as his own control. McCord, et al. (1962) investigated the effects of certain environmental factors on the subsequent development of dependent behavior in boys. Data from a longitudinal experiment dealing with the influence of intensive counseling as a deterrent to delinquency were used for this study. On the basis of rated dependency behavior in four areas (striving for adult approval, relations with peers, relationship with the project counselor, and primary reference groups) 148 subjects from the original "treatment" group were chosen for analysis. These boys were then classified as extremely dependent or moderately dependent. The extremely dependent boys were further divided into adult-dependents, peer-dependents, and pervasive dependents (both adult and peer dependent). The moderately dependent boys served as controls. Based on case history material pertaining to familial environment, childhood behavior, and adult behavior, results indicated a significantly higher incidence of parental conflict and parental rejection for boys in the extremely dependent group. These boys disliked their mothers, had abnormal fears, feelings of inferiority, anxiety concerning sex, and were oral and sadistic. One antecedent to their extremely dependent behavior was punishment during childhood for dependent behavior. In adulthood, however these boys showed no more tendency to alcoholism or criminality than did the moderate dependents but were more likely to have a psychotic breakdown. The three extremely dependent sub-groups could be distinguished and identified in terms of parental behaviors. Parents of adult-dependent boys placed high demands upon their children and were strict in their restriction and supervision of them. Opposite behavior—low demands and lack of supervision and restriction—characterized parents of peer-dependent boys. Pervasively dependent boys had dominant fathers and parents who drank excessively and were aggressive. Presented here are only some of the differentiating background factors associated with dependent males in this study. Also using a longitudinal design, Kagan and Moss (1960) found that preadolescent dependency is a better predictor of adult dependency than are early school or preschool indices.

In a study by French (1964) 73 eight- to ten-year-old boys of high socioeconomic status rated each other's aggressiveness on the Peer Rating Index and answered a questionnaire measuring parental rejection of both nurturant needs and of the subject as a person. No positive relationship was found between aggression and parental rejection. In a second study private and public school boys (high vs. low sociometric status) were compared on the same variables. Again, no relationships were found within or between the two socio-economic groups.

Grossman (1965) studied the effect of parental warmth on dependency and responsiveness to social reward in children. Twenty-six mothers were interviewed, and, from the information obtained, both father and mother were subsequently rated for warmth of relationship with the child. The children were observed for dependency in a classroom situation and individually for reaction to social reinforcement in a motor task situation. It was found that boys and girls tended to react differently. That parental warmth and responsiveness to social reward would bear a negative relationship was supported only for boys. The predicted negative correlation between parental warmth and dependency was supported only when the father had a reportedly warm relationship with his daughter. Moreover, children who behaved more dependently in the classroom responded to a greater extent to social reward only initially on the motor task.

Lovinger (1968) studied dependency, self-concept, and sense of competence among 110 middle class children at the kindergarten level and again at the first grade level. Findings indicated that for both males and females self-concept (measured by the Creelman Self-Concept Scale) and dependency (measured by the Beller Dependency Scales) were not related at the kindergarten level: interestingly, for both boys and girls, dependency and sense of competency (measured by the Moriarty Scale for Sense-of-Competence) were positively related at the kindergarten level, whereas the reverse was predicted. For males, but not for females, kindergarten dependency was positively related to first grade reading (Metropolitan Achievement Test). Further, dependency and self concept were positively related for first grade girls but not for boys; dependency and sense of competence were not related for either boys or girls at the first grade level. Finally, first grade dependency was negatively related to reading achievement for boys.

Long, et al. (1967) investigated changes in self-concept as a function of age among 373 elementary school children. Based on the assumption that the development of a sense of identity stems from experience gained from interpersonal relationships, it was predicted that individuation (self as different from others) would increase and social dependency (self as separate from the group) would decrease as a function of age. In order to test this hypothesis, first through sixth graders were administered nonverbal measures of individuation and social dependency. The results confirmed the prediction that individuation was positively related to grade in school; contrary to expectations, however, social dependency was found to increase with grade in school. The latter was discussed in terms of an increased availability of group activities and, consequently, a greater orientation toward the group for the older children. Studies by Craddock et al. (1970) with disadvantaged ghettoized minority group adults suggest that as self concept increases dependency decreases.

Acceptance by one's peers may, even in childhood, influence to some extent overt manifestations of dependency. Through the use of sociometric techniques and teacher ratings, Marshall and McCandless (1957) obtained data pertaining to dependency upon adults and patterns of peer group interaction among preschoolers. Negative correlations were found between nearly all measures of adult dependency and peer group acceptance.

Utilizing emotionally disturbed children, Beller (1957) investigated the relationships among dependency striving, autonomous achievement striving, anality, and orality. Of the 49 problem children observed, 16 were severely disturbed; eight were twins. Ages ranged from two to six years. Beller's five scales of dependency striving and five scales of autonomous achievement striving (obtaining work satisfaction, attempts to do routine tasks alone, overcome obstacles alone, initiate activity, and complete activity) were used to identify and measure dependent and autonomous behavior in the nursery school setting. These measures were then correlated with behavioral manifestations of oral (drooling, biting, etc.) and anal (retaining, etc.) activity. As predicted, autonomous achievement striving was negatively related to orality and anality, significantly to the latter. Dependency striving was found to be positively related to orality and anality, significantly with the former. When the severely disturbed and twins were eliminated from the sample, the correlation between orality and dependency was increased. These subgroups, therefore, tended to be less orally dependent. In both subgroups it may be speculated that less need satisfaction was derived from the adult and peer worlds. Twins depended to a great extent on each other; the emotionally disturbed invested much of their available energy in themselves (See Winestine, p. 77).

Having found in a previous study that dependency among children correlated more strongly with perceptual orientation toward people while autonomous achievement striving correlated more strongly with orientation toward physical objects, Beller and Turner (1964) investigated dependency and autonomous achievement striving in relation to accuracy of perceptual judgments of significant adults (i.e., mother, father, teacher) and self among 14 pre-school children. A secondary consideration was to ascertain whether autonomous achievement striving would correlate more accurately with perception when the method of measurement deemphasized the emotional context of the interpersonal relationships.

The children were tested both in the nursery and in an unfamiliar experimental room. They were required to adjust the height of a horizontal bar which could be extended mechanically until it matched the height of a group of boxes. The children were also asked to indicate when the bar and boxes were as big as mother, father, teacher, therapist, and self. The children were also asked to indicate when projected images of persons of varied sizes on a screen were as big as mother, father, etc. Response measures used were accuracy and overestimation.

For accuracy, regardless of other variables, judgment with the bar was significantly better than judgment with the picture. This could be viewed as a result of the de-emphasis of emotional context of the interpersonal relationships. Autonomous achievement striving was significantly related to accuracy of judgment in the bar-nursery situation only. For both error and accuracy data the main effect due to object was significant. An analysis of sex differences showed that boys tended to overestimate the size of the father while girls showed no overestimation of any figure. This was interpreted as indicating earlier sex typing among males than females. Only in the experimental room was there a high correlation between high dependency strivers and a tendency to overestimate the size of the mother and teacher. No other interactions between personality variables of dependency and autonomous achievement striving and experimental variables of familiarity of place, method of judgment, and object were significant.

Conformity

It appears that conformity is one response indicative of dependency. One frequently used design is that pioneered by Asch and his associates (1940). The subject is strategically placed among confederates in a social group situation and each is instructed to give verbal judgment in the presence of the others. The confederates on "critical" trials unanimously give incorrect responses. The extent to which the subject submits to group pressure on such trials is the measure of conformity behavior.

The relationship between dependency and conformity was studied by Kagan and Mussen (1956). Male college students who responded with a greater frequency of dependency themes on the TAT yielded significantly more to group opinion in an Asch-type situation than did subjects scoring less dependent. Kagan and Mussen's finding that there is a relationship between dependency and conformity suggests that a more directive type of counseling could be attempted with the more dependent rehabilitation clients.

In an effort to measure the relationship between conformity behavior and several personality variables Levy (1959) administered the EPPS, the Social Anxiety Scale, and the Social Desirability Scale. Subjects were then placed in individual booths and given multiple-choice problems to solve as in the standard Crutchfield conformity situation. Results indicated that those scoring higher on the nurturance and affiliation scales on the EPPS conformed significantly more to social pressure than subjects scoring lower. Trends only were established for other scale variables. It was suggested that the lack of significance might be attributed to the difference in social pressure in the Crutchfield as opposed to the Asch situation. In the latter, subjects render judgment verbally and in the presence of each other; the pressure to conform is, therefore, greater than when judgment is given more or less anonymously as is done in the Crutchfield situation.

A somewhat different approach to the concept of dependency was taken by Brudbard (1964). He postulated that an individual who scores low on dependency is, in fact, as dependent as one who scores high; only the mode of handling dependency needs differs. In his study he attempted to show how measures of dependency might vary with the changes in the subject's focus of attention.

Ninety-nine college students were given the Navran Scale and were subsequently classified into three groups: deniers (low scorers), flexibles (medium scorers), and acceptors (high scorers). Two Crutchfield conformity tasks, one employing geometric figures and the other vocabulary words, were presented. Directly following the experimental session, subjects were asked to evaluate their performance. The hypothesis that dependency acceptors would conform more to group pressure than the dependency flexibles was supported for geometric figures, but not for vocabulary words. Both acceptors and deniers took longer to respond on both tasks than did the flexibles. For performance evaluation, underestimation of conformity behavior was evidenced by the dependency acceptors, not the dependency deniers as had been predicted.

Flanders, et al. (1961) constructed a 45-item scale to measure dependency proneness and its relationship to student-teacher patterns of interaction. Based on the responses of eighth graders, the authors found that boys showed significantly less conformity and compliance behavior than girls and required less support and reassurance from the teacher. Their theory suggests that dependency-prone students will try to make responses which they think the teacher wants.

Zuckerman (1958), by means of peer ratings, classed 63 student nurses as rebellious, submissive, conforming or dependent (the latter three groups comprised the general class of dependents). By combining scores on the deference, succorance, and abasement scales of the EPPS, "rebellious" nurses were found to have scored significantly lower than did the "dependent" nurses. A similar analysis, utilizing combined scores from the autonomy, dominance, and aggression scales, resulted in significantly higher totals for the rebellious than for the dependent groups.

Gerai (1959) administered two forms of an 18-item Crime Questionnaire to 60 subjects equally divided among four experimental groups and a control group. The first form was a written test; the second form, an oral test. Influence attempts which were interposed between the two administrations were varied for the four experimental groups. The Direct Independence-Appeals group (DI) was instructed to give judgments not necessarily in agreement with anyone else. The Direct Conformity Appeals group (DC) was instructed to give judgments not necessarily different from that of anyone else. The Indirect Independence Appeals group (II) was given an essay and questions to answer regarding its content—strong arguments for independence. The Indirect Conformity group (IC) was presented the same questions as group II but without the essay. The control group simply took the written and oral forms of the Crime Questionnaire. Subjects were instructed to render sentence for particular crimes; on 12 of 18 crime questions the 5 or 6 stooges conferred light sentences on serious crimes and vice versa. As predicted, the IC group showed significantly greater conformity than groups DI, II, and C; group DC showed significantly greater conformity than group C, but only a trend toward greater conformity over groups DI and II. Indirect methods of conformity appeals were concluded to be more effective than direct methods; conformity appeals were more effective than independence appeals, the latter resembling the no-appeals or control group.

Kasl et al. (1959) approached the study of conformity behavior from a field theory point of view. Need for dependency was conceptualized as minimum freedom from others; need for independence, as maximum freedom from others. Independence could be achieved in either of two ways: by approaching independence or by avoiding dependence. It was predicted that conformity behavior would be resisted most by those whose need for independence was greater than need for dependence. Some months earlier 88 female undergraduates were classified as emotionally dependent, task dependent, or independent on the basis of a self-report questionnaire and tested in both an ego-involving and non-ego-involving conformity situation. An influencer intervened during both tasks for the purpose of exercising control over subject judgment. Half the subjects were informed that the influencer was incompetent and constituted the experimental group; the other half were told nothing about the qualifications of the influencer and served as controls. Task dependency was related positively to conformity but only for the ego-involving task. In the present study 51 of the original 88 subjects were reclassified for dependency on the basis of the Test of Insight. Approach-independence, approach-dependence, avoid-dependence, and avoid-independence groups were obtained by rating the behaviors of persons in various story situations as projected by the subjects. It was found that only independents in the approach-independence group conformed less, again only in the ego-involving task. The experimental groups conformed significantly less than did the controls. No relationship was established between the self-report measure of dependency and the Test of Insight.

Others, however, have obtained meaningful correlations between overt and covert indices of dependency. Zuckerman and Grosz (1958), using the Sway Test to determine high and low hypnotizability ("primary suggestibility"), demonstrated that highly suggestible student nurses scored significantly higher on succorance on the TAT than did less suggestible nurses.

In experimental situations, a direct relationship between dependent behavior and suggestibility has been demonstrated. Jakubczak and Walters (1959) exposed two groups of 9-year-old boys, high and low in dependency as determined by the Kescher scale, to the autokinetic effect. Contrary judgments by both adults and peers as to the location of a pinpoint of light were given. It was found that the high dependency group was influenced to a significantly greater extent by judgments of others than was the low dependency group. When the relative effects of adults and peer judgment were analyzed, only suggestions given by adults significantly influenced subject behavior in the high dependency group. In addition, the high dependency group was significantly more willing to accept help.

Hirsch and Singer (1961) administered to a group of chronic rebellious and to a group of nonrebellious adolescent females a series of situations involving conflict between teen-agers and authority figures. Subjects were instructed to indicate who was "in the right" or to withhold judgment. The nonrebellious group tended to side with the authorities while the rebellious group tended to side with the adolescents. However, the nonrebellious females noticed the paucity of information and revealed a lack of confidence concerning their judgments. On the other hand, the rebellious group, who identified with their peer group, tended not to recognize the lack of information in the situation presented and consequently felt more confident in their judgments.

Using the MMPI, Gough's Adjective Check List, General Maladjustment Scale, Welsh Figure Preference Scale, and a questionnaire, Barron (1953) utilized an experimental situation to determine personality correlates of independent judgment. He found that, in a general way, individuals who showed independence of judgment were original, emotional, artistic, preferred complexity, were creative, formed close interpersonal relationships, and were individual rather than group oriented. Yielders to group pressures, on the other hand, were obliging, optimistic, efficient, determined, patient, kind, practical, preferred simplicity, and were oriented to the group.

After administering to 72 college students a self-report inventory from which a measure of dependency was obtained, Tongas (1965) assigned half of the high and half of the low dependents to a "help" condition and the remaining half of each dependency group to a "withdrawal of help" condition. For the "help" condition subjects received assistance for the entire 20 minutes in solving a highly difficult problem; for the "withdrawal of help" condition subjects received assistance for the first 10 minutes only. The latter was considered to be the dependency-arousal condition. In addition, subjects were given an index measuring persuasibility both before and after the experimental session. Results indicated that high dependents scored higher on persuasibility than did low dependents. The dependency-arousal condition did not produce significantly higher persuasibility scorers as was expected. However, high dependents were found to have more increase in persuasibility than the low dependents in the arousal condition.

Rather than viewing conformity as a personality characteristic, increasing attention has been given to conformity as an instrumental response, subject to change according to laws of conditioning. Sistrunk (1969) divided 40 male college students into conformers and independents or nonconformers on the basis of their performance on a standard conformity task. Subjects were then placed in a second conformity situation in which half of the conformers and independents were reinforced for conformity behavior and the remaining half for nonconformity. As might be expected, conformers conditioned to nonconformity while independents did not condition to conformity. Conformers reinforced for conformity did not become more conforming; however, nonconformers reinforced for nonconformity evidenced increased nonconformity behavior. Spiegel and Litrownik (1968) proposed that conformity behavior cannot be predicted upon the basis of broad personality groupings (e.g., normals, schizophrenics, etc.) but, rather, that conformity will vary as a function of the dependency and self-assertiveness of the individual group members. The Spiegel Personality Inventory was administered to 76 hospitalized male schizophrenics from which two groups of 8 subjects were selected for comparison in modified Asch-type conformity situations. The two groups were characterized by high dependency-low assertiveness and low dependency-high assertiveness. Low dependent-high assertive patients were found to be significantly less conforming; thus, the importance of these factors relative to diagnostic classification was demonstrated.

Reinforcement, Anxiety, and Dependency Arousal

Use of the reward situation and the response it elicits from dependent populations has been a popular area of investigation. In their work with pre-school children, Endsley and Hartup (1960) demonstrated that highly and moderately dependent subjects were significantly more task persistent when socially reinforced than were low dependent subjects.

Cairns and Lewis (1962) differentiated high and low dependents on the basis of EPPS responses. Subjects were administered the Interpersonal Checklist for a self-reported measure of dependency and the Behavioral Dependency Test for which requests for help and time of such requests were recorded. Cards containing pronouns and verbs of dependency, aggression, and neutrality were then presented, and the subjects were instructed to make up a sentence using a pronoun and one of the three verbs. Use of one of the three verbs was reinforced with verbal approval by the experimenter for each subgroup of high dependents. After the experimental task was completed, subjects were asked to rate their feelings toward the use of such reinforcement. Subjects who regarded the reinforcement in a positive way conditioned to a higher level than subjects who assigned a negative rating to the use of verbal approval. However, there were no overall differences between high and low dependency groups for level of conditioning or for rating direction for reinforcement. A marginally significant shorter response latency was provided by the high dependents to the Behavioral Dependency Test. Dependency as determined from the EPPS was significantly related to Interpersonal Checklist items measuring dependency.

The relative effectiveness of social, material, and social-material rewards has been investigated. Walters and Foote (1962) explored the relationship between dependency, anxiety, and reward type on the discrimination learning of second grade girls. Subjects were rated by teachers on dependency striving using the Beller scales and then conditioned either in an atmosphere of anxiety or one of relaxation. Three types of reward were used to motivate performance: token plus reward, token only, and verbal approval. Although differences in performance due to levels of dependency and anxiety were in the predicted direction, neither reached significance. However, the Trials X Reward Type and the Dependency X Anxiety X Reward Type X Trials interactions were significant. When results were analyzed in terms of increases from baseline trials to the last four trials or from the first five to the last five trials, the two material rewards proved to motivate performance significantly better than verbal reward.

Bernardin and Jessor (1957) tested three postulated correlates of dependency in a construct validation experiment. Dependency was measured by the EPPS and defined as the score at or above the 70th percentile on deference and at or below the 50th percentile on autonomy with a minimum of 30 points between. Independence was defined similarly but in the opposite direction. Four groups of subjects were utilized in the first experiment: experimental-independent, experimental-dependent, control-independent, and control-dependent. The experimental groups received negative verbal reinforcement while the control groups received none. As predicted, the experimental-dependent group responded negatively to critical comments; this group made significantly more errors, took significantly longer, and evidenced significantly less savings on a maze task than did the control-dependent and experimental-independent groups. The second proposed behavioral correlate of dependency—reliance on others for help—differentiated the independent and dependent groups, the latter requesting help and reassurance significantly more often. That conformity to group opinion would be greater for the dependent group than for the independent group was not supported.

The results of a verbal conditioning study done by Stewart and Resnick (1970) has implications for the rehabilitation of delinquent boys. Thirty-three delinquents serving sentences (all of whom had been convicted on at least three previous occasions) and 33 nondelinquent boys from a nearby high school, matched for age, race, intelligence, reading and socio-economic levels, were presented cards, each containing a dependent, an aggressive, and neutral verb (e.g. depended, stabbed, scrubbed) and were requested to use one of the three verbs in a sentence. Their choice of verb on the first 20 cards was nonreinforced (operant trials); their choice of an aggressive or dependent verb on subsequent cards was reinforced (conditioning trials). The nondelinquents used dependent verbs and dependent relative to aggressive verbs significantly more frequently during the conditioning than on the operant trials; the delinquent boys showed no such increases in verb use from the operant to the conditioning trials. The authors suggested that, since traditional therapy involves a certain amount of client dependency on his therapist and stresses the client's ability to verbally communicate his feelings, conventional therapy may well fail with the delinquent whose past history is replete with negative reinforcement for dependency. This study suggests the value of the rehabilitation counselor's recognition that the rejection of a dependent relationship by their delinquent clients may not necessarily be a rejection of the counselor himself or even treatment. Thus, this knowledge enables the therapist to tolerate early discouragement rather than brand the delinquent as nonamenable to counseling.

The direct effect of anxiety on dependency was studied by Rosenthal (1965). She explored the generalization of dependency behavior from mother to stranger under two anxiety conditions. Sixty-four 3- to 5-year-old girls were classified as high or low dependent. Half of each dependency group was assigned to a high anxiety situation and half to a low anxiety situation. Each child was observed twice, once with its mother and once with a stranger. All three hypotheses were supported. Regardless of anxiety condition or level of dependency, the mother's presence produced more dependent behavior than the presence of the stranger. The high anxiety condition elicited more dependent behavior regardless of whether the mother or stranger was present. Finally, highly dependent children displayed more dependent behavior toward the stranger than did children less dependent upon their mother.

Measures of dependency-anxiety have been obtained through ratings and projectives in order to study the interactional effect of dependency and anxiety on responsiveness to reinforcement. The effect of social approval on the performance of dependent-anxious subjects was tested by Cairns (1960). Dependency-anxiety ratings (based on both overt behavior and data from an incomplete stories test) were obtained for a group of adolescent boys. Verbal reinforcement reduced overall performance of dependent-anxious subjects on three experimental tasks. These boys ultimately conditioned to a lower level in a paired-associates learning situation, conditioned less well and actually dropped in performance with increased reinforcement over trials when confiding responses in an interview situation were socially rewarded. Both groups sought less help and rejected help when offered in a highly difficult problem situation. It would appear that for individuals in conflict over dependency needs, help or approval offered by others only serves to increase anxiety which in turn interferes with performance.

On the basis of consistent ratings on the Incomplete Story Test, and insoluble form-board puzzle, and ratings of ward behavior, Goldman (1965) identified 36 hospitalized schizophrenics as high dependent and another 36 as high dependent-anxious. Subjects were presented four lists of paired-associates and on the second list, introduced to social reward, social punishment, or non-evaluation. By list four the differential effects of reward were essentially non-existent. However, earlier in the learning process it was evident that the dependent-anxious subjects performed less well under reward conditions where conflict over dependency needs was aroused and superior to non-anxious dependents under mild punishment. Under neutral conditions there was no difference between the dependency groups.

An alternative to defining anxiety in terms of ratings or test results obtained prior to the experimental task consists of manipulating the anxiety variable experimentally. The influence of approval rewards on the performance of independent and dependent emotionally disturbed preschoolers was investigated by Adler (1962). Following teacher ratings of dependency striving, the children underwent, at two different times, ten minutes of attention deprivation and ten minutes of attention saturation at the hands of the experimenter. After each such session with the experimenter, subjects were given a choice task to perform. For every correct response half of the rated high dependents and half of the rated low dependents were reinforced with verbal approval; the other half of each group received only the reinforcement of knowing they were correct. Results showed that situationally-induced dependence or independence (deprivation or saturation) had no effect on performance. However, characteristically dependent and independent children (categorized by teacher ratings of classroom behavior) were influenced by reward. High dependents who were rewarded made significantly fewer errors and improved performance at a faster rate than did high dependents who were not rewarded. Children rated low on dependency showed no differential performance rate due to reinforcement and performed midway between the high dependency groups. The results were discussed with respect to the differential response to type of reward among dependents and independents.

Through experimental manipulation Hurvitch (1960) was able to arouse the dependency need in subjects by presenting to them written material containing dependency-related events. For one group the dependency needs of the hero in the story were met (positive outcome group); for a second group the dependency needs of the hero were denied or frustrated (negative outcome group). A control group was given similar passages but containing no dependency-related events. All subjects were then asked to give stories to TAT cards. Subjects in the positive outcome group produced more dependency-related imagery on the TAT than subjects in the negative outcome group; the difference, however, was significant only for males.

Persons with heightened dependency needs tend to feel highly anxious when nurturance is absent or withdrawn. Such anxiety serves to facilitate simple task performance but interferes with performance on complex tasks. Hartup (1958) hypothesized that withdrawal of nurturance would facilitate the learning of simple tasks when performance was rewarded by verbal approval from the experimenter. Thirty-four middle to upper class preschool boys and girls received either a 10-minute period of nurturance (experimenter showed affection, approval, etc.) or a 5-minute period of nurturance followed by a 5-minute period of nurturance-withdrawal (experimenter ceased to interact with the child) prior to the presentation of tasks. In addition, ratings of the children's dependency behavior within the classroom and laboratory situations were obtained. The hypothesis was generally supported and was interpreted in terms of the child's effort to restore the previously experienced nurturant relationship with the experimenter. No significant interactions were found for levels of dependency and the treatment conditions.

DiBartolo and Vinacke (1969) instructed teachers to rate their pupils, participants in a federally sponsored preschool program for socially and economically disadvantaged families, on dependency using the Beller scales. Twelve boys and 12 girls, divided into high and low dependency groups, were randomly assigned to a nurturance or nurturance-deprivation setting in which their task was to solve a complex puzzle. As predicted, children rated high on dependency and who received no praise, verbal affection, or other nurturance performed significantly more poorly than did the other three groups.

The effects of characteristic dependency and experimentally induced dependency stress on the task performance of 88 kindergarteners were studied by Newcomer (1968). Characteristic dependency was determined by ratings of the children's behavior within the kindergarten setting. High dependency stress was defined as social deprivation and low stress as social reward during a 15-minute period prior to a learning task on which correct performance was verbally reinforced. The children were assigned to one of four task (easy vs. difficult) -stress (low vs. high) conditions. Results confirmed the hypothesis. Low dependent children performed better on both tasks under high dependency stress than under low dependency stress: the increased drive and the resultant increased effectiveness of the reinforcement contributed to better learning. On the other hand, on the complex task only, the performance of high dependent children suffered under high dependency stress: apparently the drive was increased beyond the point for good performance and with poor performance less reinforcement was possible.

Experimentation has shown the need of dependent subjects for a more formalized environment in which to function. Kuenzli (1959) administered to a group of 100 college students items involving controversial subject matter. Among the items the following was used to differentiate students who favor high structure from students who favor low structure situations: "It is essential for learning or effective work that our teachers or bosses outline in detail what is to be done and exactly how to go about it." Thirty-three subjects "agreed" or "strongly agreed" with the item and were placed in the high structure group; 67 subjects "disagreed" or "strongly disagreed" with the item and were placed in the low structure group. Following testing the subjects filled out a personal data sheet containing items, among others, concerning religious preference, family income, college major, political leanings, marital status, and hometown population. Analysis indicated significant differences for most of the items for the two groups. The concept of dependency was proposed to account for the results. It was suggested that an individual who prefers high structure is one who tends to be "less mature, less confident, less differentiated in cognitive experiences."

Potanin (1959) studied the effects of experimentally induced stress on perceptual variables of depth and detail in relation to the personality variables of dependency, insecurity, and anxiety. Male undergraduates were divided into high, medium, and low groups for acknowledged dependency and insecurity on the basis of the Taylor Manifest Anxiety Scale. Preference for detail and depth was measured at each of two sessions. Half of the subjects were informed after the second session that they scored on the borderline of the Masculinity-Femininity subscale of the MMPI and constituted the stress group for the second session; half of the remaining subjects were told that they scored on the masculine end of the distribution and served as controls along with subjects who did not take the MMPI subscale until the end of the second session. A significant difference resulted among the dependency groups with respect to preference for detail on the first session before stress was introduced, with high dependency groups preferring greater detail. However, the change in preference for detail after stress was introduced was significantly related only to insecurity. Detail was more preferred under stress by the low insecurity group and less preferred by the medium insecurity group; the high insecurity group showed no change. Change in preference for depth was related only to level of anxiety. Low anxiety subjects increased their preference for depth under stress while medium and high anxious subjects evidenced no change in depth preference.

The effect of psychological factors on perceived physical sensation may be of use in determining the extent to which an individual is dependent. Collins (1965) surveyed a sample of 62 U.S. soldiers with Childhood History Question-naires for which each subject rated himself for protection, independence, and stimulation (new experience, change, etc.). The sample was then tested for pain sensitivity by increases in intensity of electric shock to two fingers. A positive correlation was found between protection and pain threshold as well as between protection and pain tolerance. Independence correlated negatively with both pain scores. No relationship existed between stimulation and pain scores. It was concluded that sensitivity to pain was greater in adulthood when pain was experienced to a greater extent in childhood.

In an experiment by Lahtinen (1964) dependency as a function of fear of failure and fear of rejection was studied. Kindergarten children were assigned to one of three groups: failure-arousal, rejection-arousal, and neutral. A story completion test provided an index of covert dependency manifestation; a difficult puzzle presented during the experimental session served as an index of overt dependency manifestation. Both failure and rejection groups exhibited more dependent behavior, both overt and covert, than did the neutral group. The prediction that more counterdependent behavior would be evidenced by the failure group was generally not supported. Dependency for girls increased to a greater extent under the rejection condition than the failure, but there was no difference between the two conditions for boys.

Sentence completions are similarly used to obtain covert behavioral mani-festations. Naylor (1956) investigated the relationship between problem solving ability and dependency. The TAT and Incomplete Sentence Blank (ISB) obtained from a group of college students were scored for need value and freedom of movement; a measure of dependency was obtained from the ISB only. According to Rotter's social learning theory, persons whose need value is high and whose freedom of movement is low would be more apt to depend upon others for assistance and be less efficient in a problem solving situation than persons whose need value is low and whose freedom of movement is high. Time to solve the problem, frequency of questions asked the experimenter, and self-depreciating remarks made while working at the problem were recorded. The proposed hypothesis concerning dependent behavior in a problem-solving situation was supported by ISB but not by TAT data. When dependency and freedom of movement were held constant, subjects scoring high on need value tended to make self-depreciating remarks and asked more questions than subjects scoring low on need value. When dependency and need value were held constant, subjects scoring low on freedom of movement produced significantly more dependency responses than subjects scoring high on freedom of movement. Without considering need value and freedom of movement, however, ISB dependency did not relate to dependent behavior. A nonsignificant positive relationship was found between problem-solving time and dependency behavior when level of intelligence was controlled.

Dependency in Small Group Situations

Although a detailed consideration of the exercise of power is beyond the scope of this book, it must be noted that such variables as the manipulation of power may influence exhibited dependency. In the following studies it is shown that artificial dependency may be created through communication within a group structure. For a more detailed consideration of these forces the reader is referred to Cartwright and Zandar (1962) and Hare, Borgatta, and Bales (1955).

In a study by Jones et al. (1963) 150 male undergraduates listened to taped opinion interchanges between two students, A and B, the latter always expressing his opinions second. Two agreement conditions, close and variable, were established by varying the degree of agreement of B with A. Half of the subjects were instructed that compatibility of response was important in that it would determine whether or not the two students would take part in another experiment; the remaining half were told that compatibility of response was not important. After listening to the opinion interchange, subjects evaluated on a 12-point scale the agreement of B with A from two positions of reference: the subject as a bystander and as the student whose opinion was presented first. Results showed that subjects evaluated B more negatively than they did their evaluation of A's reaction to B. Their estimated evaluation of B was higher when agreement was less and lower when agreement was close. Differences due to dependency conditions were not significant for either evaluation, but the interaction between dependency and agreement was for S's own evaluation of B. For variable agreement, subjects in the high dependency condition, where compatibility of response was important, evaluated B significantly more negatively than did subjects in the low dependency condition. For close agreement, subjects in the high dependency condition were significantly less negative in their evaluation of B than were subjects in the low dependency condition.

Schellenberg (1965) employed college students in a decision-making situation. The object of the game, the subject was told, was to accrue the maximum number of points possible. An alternative, evident as the game progressed, was to obtain a joint maximum of points totaling more than the maximum which could be obtained individually. It was found that if either of the two parties selected the alternative approach or made choices dependent upon the other's choice, there occurred an increase in collaboration between the two (joint maximum of points) and a decrease in exploitation (maximum of points for one at the expense of another) and in disengagement (assured, but less than maximum, number of points).

An interesting approach to the study of dependency was an experiment by Schopler and Bateson (1965). Their purpose was to study the yield of a powerful person to the dependency of his powerless "partner." In the first of three experiments dependency was defined in terms of time pressure: for a high dependency group a Ph.D. candidate requested summer student volunteers for an experiment to be completed that summer; for a low dependency group, completion by the following summer. As in all three experiments the experimenter assumed the role of the powerless person dependent upon others for the attainment of some goal; the others, or the subjects, were considered to be more powerful since the choice to comply with the experimenter's wishes was theirs. From analysis a marginally significant interaction effect between sex and dependency resulted, with females yielding more when the experimenter was highly dependent upon them and males yielding more when the experimenter was less dependent upon them.

In the second experiment the element of cost to the subject of yielding to his dependent partner was introduced. In a decision-making task the subject's partner (again the experimenter) sent to the subject on each trial a message expressing his preference for an alternative. Each alternative was one of four boxes containing varying amounts of numbers, a number from one box being drawn from an urn as the winning number. Dependence of the partner upon the subject was defined by the amount of money the partner could win should the subject choose the correct box of numbers. Cost to the subject of yielding to his partner's choice was defined by the probability of winning from each one of the alternatives or boxes. The high-cost-of-yielding condition represented a greater proportional loss. Eighteen of the 26 trials were "critical" trials in that the subject's least preferred alternative was the partner's choice.

Under low-cost-of-yielding, females yielded significantly more when their partner was highly dependent; males yielded significantly more when their partner was not highly dependent. Under high-cost-of-yielding, males yielded significantly more when their partner was highly dependent upon them; females showed no difference. In the third experiment the high-cost-of-yielding condition was dropped. Again, males yielded significantly more than females to the low dependency condition. Results were discussed in terms of submission to a norm of social responsibility.

Utilizing a similar design, Schopler and Mathews (1965) studied another condition affecting yielding to dependence—the perceived causal locus of the partner's dependence. Subjects in the "external locus" condition heard that their associates could complete puzzles only by requesting letters from the directors, while the subjects in the "internal locus" conditions were told that their associates had a choice between getting letters from a random pool or requesting letters from directors. It was substantiated that a powerful person who believes his partner's dependence to be caused by environmental factors will help more than a powerful person who believes his partner's dependence to be caused by personal factors.

In a situation in which the relative number of dots on two fields were judged, Phares (1965) tested 80 subjects in groups of four for compliant behavior as a function of dependence and power. Power was conceptualized as the degree to which a subject can produce the result wanted. Dependence was conceptualized as the degree to which the result wanted can be produced by another subject. Experimentally, these two variables were manipulated by varying the proportion of payoff. Subjects interacted through written message. Among other findings, compliant behavior to high power senders was found to be greatest for high dependent-low power receivers; similarly compliant behavior to low power senders was found to be less for high power-low dependent receivers.

Implications for Rehabilitation

It has been the purpose of this chapter to show and provide examples of attempts made to identify and measure dependency. Such identification and evaluation have important implications for the field of rehabilitation. If a counselor or, indeed, any rehabilitation professional is working with a client, he must have some means of evaluating the strength of dependent strivings and understanding the degree to which such strivings are blocking the rehabilitation process. Moreover, he must not be misled by the apparent independence of, in reality, dependent clients.

Expression of excessive dependency in the client is a major stumbling block to successful rehabilitation. If the practitioner is to intervene to reduce dependency, he must have some means of objectively viewing and understanding his client's dependent needs. Although it is not implied that tests are a substitute for skilled interviewing techniques, there is a need for development of criteria for the identification and estimation of the strength of the client's dependency. Of equal importance is the need for development of a method for differentiating true dependent strivings from those evoked due to conflict over dependency.

Findings have suggested a positive relationship between degree of dependence and suggestibility. If suggestibility is associated with dependency, the counselor can, to some extent, compensate for dependence in the client by the judicious use of suggestion which will be accepted by the client. This is another way of saying that the client who shows high dependence might benefit by more directive counseling techniques. However, the rehabilitation practitioner must remain aware of his influence on clients. If the dependency-prone client constantly responds in a manner related to what he thinks the practitioner wants, then the practitioner's own views and ideas concerning the client's rehabilitation may be imposed on the client rather than being worked out on the basis of the client's needs and the client's participation. Thus, the identification of the dependency-prone rehabilitation client is of vital importance.

The relationship between dependency and the degree of group structure should be considered by professionals in the field. Many clients undergo experiences in the process of rehabilitation which are essentially group experiences. The sheltered workshop, the hospital, the nursing home, the rehabilitation center—all these settings involve a certain group structure. If group structure can be manipulated as a vehicle for the management of client dependency this would indeed be a step forward. Moreover, with increased use of group counseling techniques, the consideration of group structure takes on high significance. Perhaps by gradually reducing the degree of structure of the group, independence can be called forth in some individuals.

The relationship between dependency and structure, as reflected by preference for detail, could have implications in the areas of job placement and the sheltered workshop. If dependency can be assessed for a given client, the work to which he is assigned can be chosen with greater chance for success.

The use of acceptance by members of the group as a motivator to reduce dependence is a valid technique. A definite need for rewarding the dependent client has been indicated. This relationship between dependency and reward has implications not only in the process of rehabilitation counseling but in the rehabilitation center and sheltered workshop setting as well.

There is also a need for selectivity in the giving of approval and reward. While the studies reviewed suggest the importance of approval and reward to gain better performance from dependent individuals, indiscriminate use of reinforcement with clients in conflict over their dependency could serve to increase anxiety, thus blocking the rehabilitation process.

The results of some studies suggested that there are certain background factors in the lives of subjects which are associated with dependent behavior. An awareness of these factors by rehabilitation practitioners both in the counseling and facility settings could have value in the psychosocial transactions with clients. For example, it has been noted that children who came from large high density families were more dependent than those who came from small families of less high density. Also, children whose mothers died early in their lives (before four years of age) were found to be more dependent in adulthood than those who lost their mothers later (11-17 years). In addition, it has been suggested that first born and only children may be more dependent. Such factors as parental rejection, and inconsistency in reaction to and punishment of dependent behavior have been shown to be associated with dependent behavior later in life. Further investigation of these factors as they relate to the progress of the client in the rehabilitation process are necessary so that the practitioner can be prepared to take appropriate interventive action to counter inappropriate dependency strivings.

Looking at overdependency as a product of excessive oral fixation, the relationship between orality and dependency has significant implications for the process of rehabilitation. The rehabilitation practitioner who is able to recognize oral characteristics in his clients is in a good position to deal with their inappropriate dependency. The oral client who is demanding and aggressive can be helped to learn to give of himself in the rehabilitation process as well as to constantly attempt to satisfy his own needs. Dealing with dependency in the oral character is difficult. Yet, positive changes are possible when rehabilitation activities are geared toward the achievement of this goal, particularly group participation activities in which the client is required to contribute to the mutual benefit of others. In this way the oral dependent client dilutes his dependent relationships so that dependence can become interdependence and finally independence.

Of particular importance is the finding that anxiety leads to greater dependence in dependent persons. Thus, any actions on the part of the rehabilitation professional which stimulates undue anxiety in the client can impede or even defeat the rehabilitation process. Moreover, it has been found that dependent individuals who are in a state of anxiety perform less well under reward conditions. This finding has important implications in maintaining the therapeutic milieu of sheltered workshops and rehabilitation centers.

Studies have shown quite conclusively that conformity and persuasibility are positively related to dependency. This knowledge is important for the practitioner of rehabilitation since it advances the possibility of a more directive approach in the manipulation of client activities. It is also important for the counselor or rehabilitation therapist to note that studies suggest, although not conclusively, that females are more conforming than males.

4

Field Dependence:
A Perceptual Approach

For the past two decades H.A. Witkin and his associates have devoted considerable attention to the study of individual differences in patterns of adaptation as a function of cognitive style. Their theoretical framework is built around the concept of differentiation. Differentiation refers to the structural (vs. the content) aspects of a system, whether that system be psychological, social, or biological. Within a psychological system, differentiation denotes the complexity of that system in terms of the degree of separation of component parts (i.e. feelings, thoughts, needs, behavior, etc.) and specificity of function. It does not imply effective integration of parts. Since rehabilitation demands that the client interact with a number of psychosocial systems (i.e. family, vocational, etc.) (Olshansky and Margolin, 1963), the assessment and development of his capacity for differentiation and integration is likely to be crucial for the rehabilitation practitioner.

Aspects of the Differentiation Concept

Psychological differentiation refers to the ability to analyze and structure experience, both internal and external to the self. In the earlier stages of development, the infant is relatively undifferentiated; i.e., he is unable to distinguish his own body from the external world. As development progresses, the child becomes increasingly more aware of a difference between himself and his environment, more able to differentiate among the various parts of his body and their specific functions, more able to differentiate among the various aspects of his environment and their relation to each other and to himself.

The role of the mother is presumably quite crucial in determining level of differentiation, for the degree to which she is able to allow her child to separate from her and function in a relatively independent manner undoubtedly affects his potential for developing an adequate sense of self, one aspect of psychological differentiation. The child develops a sense of self through experiences with his parents and significant others in his milieu and through experiences with the external world about him. He imitates, identifies with and internalizes certain attributes and values and thus comes to perceive himself as a unique individual, both like and unlike other individuals.

A person who has developed an adequate sense of self has his own resources and frames of reference available for use in relating to others and to the environment. The extent to which a person is relatively able to rely upon his own resources rather than to rely upon other people or allow the external environment to play a significant role in determining his attitudes and behavior is the extent to which he is differentiated or field independent. Witkin and his colleagues suggested three areas of behavior for study which might be said to reflect a sense of separate identity: the amount of help and support needed from other people, the extent to which others are able to exert their influence to effect change in attitudes and values, and the extent to which the external situation or circumstance is permitted to influence self-definition.

In their book, *Psychological Differentiation*, Witkin, Dyk, Fatherson, Goodenough, and Karp (1962) discuss in detail these concepts, bring in related literature, and, in general, provide an excellent orientation to the field of perceptual dependency. Three tests have been developed to measure field dependence; the Rod-And-Frame (RFT), the Body Adjustment (BAT), and the Embedded Figures (EFT). Each requires that the subject separate an item—a rod, his own body, or a geometric figure—from its surroundings. Field dependency situations involve "perceiving an object in relation to its surrounding or a part within a larger whole. . . . Whereas for some people perception of the part was strongly affected by the surrounding field, others were able to escape this influence and to deal with the part as a more or less independent unit" (Witkin, 1950).

Thus, during the process of rehabilitation when the client is being helped to adjust to his handicap (physical, emotional, or social) it is important for the practitioner to consider internal factors as well as the client's perceptual field. For example, the individual who becomes paraplegic probably becomes principally concerned with that part of his perceptual field which is close in and related to concrete need satisfactions directly affected by his dramatically reduced motor capacity. Whereas his perceptual field may have once included an entire world, his current field may be reduced to the life space related to his body (at least until he adjusts).

Research Involving the Differentiation Concept

After 15 years of promising research, Witkin stated that "research on cognitive styles . . . has important implications for personality theory, research, problems of diagnosis, and therapy." The studies to be presented here generally include those published after 1962, but the vast amount of research done utilizing the differentiation hypothesis necessitated inclusion of only those studies believed by the authors to be of greatest interest to those in the field of rehabilitation.

One aspect of differentiation is articulation of the body. This concept refers to an awareness of the separate parts of the body as well as their interrelations and an awareness of the boundaries of the body as separate from the environment. Two studies involving the body concept will be cited; the first involves perceived bodily sensations and the second, a physically impaired body. Sweeney and Fine (1965) studied the relationship between pain tolerance and field dependency among 48 young soldiers. Subjects were grouped as high, medium, or low pain tolerators according to both perception of pain and actual skin temperature after immersion of one hand in cold water. In addition, the men were classified as perceptually dependent or perceptually independent on the basis of tests of field dependence. The hypothesis that the global or more field dependent group would show significantly higher pain tolerance than the analytical or field independent group was supported, when perceived pain data was used for analysis.

Bruel and Peszcynski (1958) administered the RFT to 42 hemiplegics, 37 neurological controls (spinal cord, multiple sclerosis, and Parkinson patients), 50 elderly normals with no known history of stroke, and 24 college students. Although field dependence increased with age among the groups, the hemiplegics scored significantly more perceptually dependent than did the neurological group even when age was controlled. That brain damage is an important contributing factor to field dependence was pointed out by the finding that perceptual dependence among hemiplegics increased as function of the number of CVAs suffered. The value of the RFT as a prognostic tool was also demonstrated. Ambulation training was found to be significantly more successful among hemiplegics who evidenced the greater degree of differentiation. Success in rehabilitation training was measured in terms of independence-dependence in both activities of daily living and bed-bound-ambulatory continuums.

The relationship between perceptual dependence and various pathologies has been investigated. Pathology can be observed in persons functioning at any level of differentiation. The ability to structure and analyze experience, both self experience and experience external to the self, does not necessarily imply effective integration of these experiences, i.e. adequate adjustment. Integration, like differentiation, is another formal aspect of personality structure and refers to the interrelationship of parts within the system and their relationship to the world external to the system. Integration can be either effective or ineffective.

Effective integration "is a more or less harmonious working together of system components with each other and of the total system with its environment, thereby contributing to the adaptation of the organism. In psychological systems effectiveness of integration is reflected in adequacy of adjustment" (Witkin et al., 1962). The form the pathology takes, however,—in the defense mechanism chosen and the symptomatic behavior exhibited—has been noted to differ among persons functioning at various levels of psychological differentiation. For example, in paranoid patients, where behaviors are oriented toward self-preservation, a field articulated (independent) approach is often found, and the highly structured defense mechanism, projection, is frequently employed. In contrast, the alcoholic deals with stress in terms of self-destruction through alcohol, a nonspecialized (or field dependent) approach.

Witkin et al. (1962) hypothesized a relationship between type of defense mechanism chosen and level of differentiation. Specifically, persons characterized by the less structured, less specialized types of defenses would be expected to perceive the world in a less structured, less differentiated manner. Ihilevich (1968) administered the Defense Measuring Instrument (DMI), the EFT and the Figure Drawing Test to 110 male and female psychiatric outpatients and 40 controls. Those who depended primarily on global or nonspecialized defenses (denial and aggression turned inward) scored more perceptually dependent than those who depended primarily on structured defense mechanisms (aggression turned outwards and projection). As would be expected, control subjects scored at an intermediate level on field dependency and preferred defenses of a corresponding (or intermediate) level of differentiation.

The differentiation hypothesis would predict that the performance of hallucinatory psychotics would be field dependent relative to that of delusional psychotics because the former patient group symptom manifestation is less structured and reflects a less well-defined sense of self. Powell (1970) employed three matched groups of 24 hospitalized psychotics equally divided for sex: "recent" auditory hallucinators, "past" auditory halluncinators, and nonhallucinators or delusional psychotics. A matched group of 24 hospital employees served as controls. Subjects were tested on the RFT, a short form of the EFT, and the vocabulary subtest of the WAIS. Results showed that the hallucinators performed significantly more field dependently than did the nonhallucinators; however, when intelligence was controlled, hallucinators did not differ from delusional patients on either the RFT or EFT. This finding indicates that the less intelligent rather than the more field dependent psychotic manifests the less differentiated symptom pattern. Control subjects tested less field dependent than the patient groups whether intelligence was eliminated as a factor or not.

Frank (1969) tested the hypothesis that moods of less differentiated persons will be characterized by a greater variability and intensity and a lesser degree of complexity, and that feelings which covary with changes in elation-depression (hedonic level) will differ for persons functioning at different levels of psychological differentiation. Fifty college students given the EFT and figure drawing tests to provide measures of perceptual dependence were asked to record their daily moods using the Personal Feeling Scales (51 mood-related indices) for a month. Other information which might be expected to affect daily mood such as physical health, amount of sleep, and pressures, was also obtained. Only mood complexity (number of factors comprising the mood) was found to be associated with perceptual dependence.

That the level of differentiation per se is not related to the presence or absence of pathology was illustrated in a study by Sugarman and Cancro (1968) based on data from an earlier study. At the time the study was conducted the authors attempted to predict hospitalization outcome at 6 months among 51 male hospitalized schizophrenics on the basis of RFT performance and the Phillips Scale of premorbid adjustment. At that time outcome was predicted correctly for 36 patients on the basis of the Phillips Scale alone whereas the RFT showed no correlation with the outcome. Upon re-examination of the data, however, outcome was predicted correctly for 39 patients on the basis of extreme RFT scores alone (a U-shaped relationship) and for 42 patients when coupled with scores from the Phillips Scale. Good prognosis was found to be associated with a moderate rather than extreme levels of psychological differentiation.

Similarly, personal adequacy as reflected by parole success might be expected to relate neither to extreme field independence nor extreme field dependence but rather to a level intermediate. Renear (1970) administered the RFT, EFT, and three subtests of the WAIS involving analytical ability to 90 inmates at a women's prison. Women who scored at a level intermediate on the EFT and on the WAIS subtests were less likely to have returned to prison. RFT performance did not differentiate returnees from nonreturnees.

Persons exhibiting certain manifest symptoms, regardless of the underlying psychodynamic processes or etiological factors involved, have been shown to exhibit similar modes of perception. For example, the behavior of alcoholics, the obese, ulcer patients, enuretics, and asthmatics is commonly regarded as symptomatic of severe dependency and/or conflict in regard to dependency. Dependency may be considered one manifestation of a relatively underdeveloped sense of separate identity and, consequently, would be expected to be characteristic of relatively field dependent persons (less differentiated).

Field Dependence and Alcohol Dependence

Derived need satisfaction from oral behavior is characteristic of the alcohol dependent personality with supposed roots in the early mother-child relationship. Using the BAT, RFT, and EFT, Witkin et al. (1959) demonstrated the field dependence component of the alcoholic personality. Even when hospitalization, certain background variables, and psychopathology were controlled, this personality characteristic persisted. The composite battery of tests was able to differentiate with greater than 75 percent accuracy the alcohol dependent from normal and psychiatric patients.

Employing 19 tuberculous patients and 19 alcoholics with tuberculosis, Rhodes and Yorioka (1968) correlated measures of field dependence (short form of the EFT) and social dependence (Dy scale of the MMPI) with alcoholism and length of hospitalization. The two all-male groups ranged in age from 30-65 and were matched for age, education, and duration of hospitalization. As predicted, alcoholics tested more dependent than nonalcoholics but only on the measure of field dependence. Longer hospitalization was reflected only by greater *social* dependence among nonalcoholics and only by greater *perceptual* dependence among alcoholics. Because of the low relationship between field and social dependence, it was again suggested that dependence not be regarded as a unitary personality trait.

Based on the premise that relative field independence is partially related to successful functioning within one's environment, Burdick (1969) administered the short form of the EFT to 21 chronic male alcoholics who were hospitalized at a private facility (the mean income of a previous sample of patients at the same hospital was $17,000). The results indicated that these alcoholics were more field independent than a control group selected for comparison. However, these findings should be viewed with caution for reasons noted by the investigator.

Bailey et al. (1961) also demonstrated with the RFT greater field dependence among groups of alcoholics (hospitalized brain damaged alcoholics) relative to their controls (AA volunteers who had been "dry" for one year). In order to determine the effects of organic damage as well as psychopathology upon performance, nonalcoholic brain-damaged, nonalcoholic paranoid schizo-phrenics, and alcoholic sociopathic patients were also administered the RFT. Again, it was observed that neither hospitalization nor the presence of pathology affected performance. However, the nonalcoholic brain-damaged group scored even more field dependent than the brain-damaged alcoholics and led to the speculation that field dependence might have resulted from prolonged heavy drinking rather than having served as a predisposing factor in alcohol de-pendence.

Goldstein & Chotlos (1965) used the RFT, among other perceptual tests, to evaluate the relationship between brain damage and dependence in 50 adult male hospitalized alcoholics. A group of 50 male adult hospital employees of approximately the same age and intelligence served as controls. They found that, while there was no striking difference in dependency between the groups, the alcoholics showed deteriorative changes in the central nervous system at a younger age.

Karp and Konstadt (1965) investigated the prolonged effect of heavy drinking on the field dependence of a group of male alcoholics who had been highly dependent upon alcohol for six years. These two groups were compared to two groups of normals whose mean ages corresponded to that of the two groups of alcoholics. As expected, the older groups were more field dependent than the younger and the alcoholic groups were more field dependent than the control groups. However, the interaction between age and alcohol dependency was not significant and was interpreted to mean that field dependence is not the result of prolonged drinking.

To determine whether the ingestion of alcohol would affect perceptual dependence, Karp et al. (1965) administered the BAT, RFT, and EFT to male alcoholics, half of whom were under the influence of alcohol during the first administration and the other half under the influence during the second administration of tests. Comparisons of first and second test scores generally indicated no change in field dependence and was interpreted as providing support for the predisposition hypothesis.

Kristofferson (1968) did a similar experiment but used, instead, non-alcoholic college students. She found, however, an increase in field dependence as reflected by the RFT post-test scores following alcohol intake. Further, the interaction between level of field dependence and change scores following alcohol intake was not significant, indicating that the effects of alcohol on performance were not differential. Kristofferson interpreted the data as supportive of the consequence hypothesis. In reference to Karp's study, she speculated that possibly after a certain amount of time the field dependence component would become relatively stable and more difficult to change and suggested that a longitudinal study might provide a more satisfactory answer to the predisposition-consequence argument.

Klappersack (1968) also questioned the predisposition hypothesis and administered various tests of visual, postural, and organizational ability to groups of hospitalized alcoholics, brain-damaged patients and controls after determining their level of field dependence based on RFT performance. The brain-damaged performed more poorly than the other groups; but the alcoholics and controls displayed similar sources of difficulty, regardless of level of field dependence. The field dependent subjects, whether alcoholics or controls, performed poorest on tests of visual organization but neither alcoholics nor field dependents performed less well on the postural tests.

The predisposition explanation of alcohol dependency was also questioned by Groden (1970). Two groups of alcoholics (short-termers and long-termers) and control groups (hospital employees matched on the basis of age and educational variables) were given the Gottschaldt HFT (sensitive to field dependence and brain damage) and the Trail Making Test (sensitive to brain damage). The alcoholics as a whole did not differ from the hospital employees on either test; however, long-term alcoholics performed significantly poorer on the HFT while short-termers performed significantly better on the Trail Making Test than their respective controls. Because long-term alcoholics evidenced both brain damage and dependency while short-termers did not, the authors concluded that HFT dependency does not predispose persons to alcohol dependency.

In order to ascertain the relative influence of field orientation, alcoholism and brain damage on RFT performance as reflected by its various components, Goldstein et al. (1970) tested groups of field independent alcoholics, field dependent alcoholics, field dependent nonalcoholics, and field dependent brain damaged nonalcoholics on postural orientation (Tilting Chair and Heath Rail-walking Tests), visual-postural skill (Rod Verticality Test), and cognitive-analytic abilities (EFT and the Block Design, Picture Completion, and Object Assembly subtests of the WAIS). Field independents performed significantly better than field dependents on all tests of visual-postural skills and cognitive-analytic abilities; the presence or absence of alcoholism played a relatively small role in test performance. The absence of significant interactions (alcoholism-nonalcoholism X field orientation) indicated that differences in performance between field dependents and field independents were independent of an alcoholism diagnosis. Field independents (regardless of diagnosis) were superior to the brain damaged nonalcoholic group on nearly all measures, while the field dependents' superiority (regardless of diagnosis) over the brain damaged was less prevalent. Thus, the predisposition vs. consequence explanations of alcohol dependency require still further investigation.

The pile-up of evidence relative to the elevated field dependence level in many alcoholics suggests the importance to the rehabilitation practitioner of manipulating the environmental resources (treatment and otherwise) to enable the alcohol dependent to clarify his own identity per se, particularly helping him delineate his own psychosocial relationship to the various elements which comprise this field. Research by Perry et al.(1970) suggested a prevalence of identity problems in alcohol dependent individuals.

Field Dependence and Other Emotionally-Based Disorders

Purportedly, dynamics similar to those involved in alcohol dependence underlie the condition of obesity. Like the alcohol dependent, the person who compulsively eats to allay anxiety or satisfy some need for dependence does so in a nonspecific fashion. Neither eating nor drinking is tied to specific stimuli and both affect experience in general. Hence, it would be expected that obese persons would perform similarly to alcoholics on measures of field dependence. Karp and Pardes (1965) gave the BAT, RFT, and EFT to obese women volunteers from a nutrition clinic and to a group of matched controls. The field dependence component of the obese personality was demonstrated and was said to reflect severe problems of dependency and inadequacy and a poorly developed sense of separate identity. Why the presenting symptom or choice of defense is different for persons with, supposedly, similar psychodynamics has yet to be determined; perhaps longitudinal study may provide some of the answers.

Asthma is another example of a condition believed to be a symptomatic manifestation of deep-seated dependency needs. If asthmatics have achieved less in the way of a separate identity and hence are more susceptible to external influences, it might be hypothesized that a change in environment for field dependent asthmatic children would result in a change in symptom. Fishbein (1963) administered the RFT and EFT to 60 chronic asthmatic patients, aged 9-15 in Denver. Although the field dependent children did show the expected decrease in symptomatic behavior following the change from family to a residential home environment, they did not differ significantly from relatively field independent children.

Operating under the same principle, Scallon & Herron (1969) predicted that a group of lower class enuretic boys from a pediatric and from a psychiatric clinic and their mothers would test relatively field dependent on the EFT. Enuretics have been clinically described as passive, dependent, and maintaining poor impulse control. Results indicated that the boys but not their mothers proved perceptually dependent. No differences were observed between the clinic groups, indicating again the lack of association between field articulation and pathology per se. In a study of persons with essential hypertension and peptic ulcers, Silverstone and Kissin (1968) found that on the basis of EFT scores peptic ulcer patients were significantly more field dependent than patients with essential hypertension but that neither differed from a group of controls.

With the exception of the study done by Silverstone and Kissin (1968), the sources from which patient groups and their controls were drawn has differed. Thus, the question was raised as to whether field dependence was related to the symptons or illnesses manifested by certain patient groups or to the sources from which groups were selected. Karp et al.(1969) administered the short form of the EFT to 20 private diabetes patients, 20 clinic diabetics, and to two groups of 20 controls matched to the private and clinic groups for age, sex, and socioeconomic status. The private and clinic groups differed for socioeconomic status. The results were as follows: diabetics performed more field dependently than controls, clinic patients and their controls performed more field dependently than private patients and their controls, and clinic diabetics tested more field dependently than private diabetics (but clinic controls did not differ from private controls). Because clinic and private patient controls did not differ, differences in field dependence between clinic and private diabetics cannot be attributed to differences in socioeconomic status. It was suggested that (for several reasons mentioned) persons who choose clinic treatment for symptom alleviation may possess greater needs for psychological support.

Using the EFT, Ruma (1967) demonstrated the dependency component believed to underlie psychosomatic illness. Adolescents suffering from psychosomatic complaints performed relatively field dependent in comparison to adolescents suffering from actual organic disease.

With intelligence controlled for, Cohn (1968) observed that among sixth grade boys and girls field dependent performance on the EFT was related to lower scores on those aspects of reading comprehension (Sangren-Woody Reading Test) which call for problem solving independent of past experience and external authority. The author stated:

We may yet learn that reading difficulty, instead of being the cause of other problems is, like them, only an effect which is the result of a kind of cognitive style that makes for less effective functioning in dealing with the total environment, of which school work is only a part.

Watson's (1970) data also supported the relationship between reading achievement and field orientation, with field independent children superior to field dependent children in the first three school grades.

As mentioned in a previous section, it is especially difficult to ascertain level of dependence by use of self report measures for persons who are in conflict over their dependence, whatever the level. The use of perceptual tests such as those developed by Witkin may provide more sensitive measuring instruments. The following study is illustrative. Gordon (1953) administered a self-report dependency scale to groups of ulcer patients, neurotics, and controls. No differences were found among groups. On the other hand, the RFT did demonstrate the field (perceptual) dependence component of the ulcer patient. The author explained this discrepancy on the basis of the commonly regarded psychodynamic picture of the ulcer patient: that of an overachieving, ambitious person who through his striving seeks to compensate for unacceptable dependency needs.

Levinson (1967) administered the short form of the EFT to 48 homeless men on skid row. Those men who were newcomers to the area and obtaining assistance from an emergency shelter tested less field dependent than those who had been living at a care facility for homeless men. Longer term institutional dependence, then, was reflected in greater perceptual dependence; in other words those who were perceptually dependent appeared to have lacked the ability to re-enter the mainstream of society.

A pilot study done by Harano (1970) yielded a significant relationship between field orientation and automobile accident involvement. Twenty-seven male accident-free drivers and 28 males who had been involved in at least three accidents over a three-year period were compared for performance on a shortened version of the EFT. Field dependency was found to be characteristic of the accident-prone group.

Field Dependence and Psychosocial Dependence

Many investigators have attempted to ascertain the relationship between perceptual dependence and other manifestations of dependence, e.g. conformity, passivity, etc. In general, paper-and-pencil tests of psychological and social dependence have either failed to relate consistently or to relate at all to measures of perceptual dependence.

One might expect that persons who are able to deal actively with their environment would have achieved a higher degree of differentiation than those who relate to their external world in a largely passive capacity. Marlowe (1958) hypothesized that (Gottschaldt) EFT performance, when field independent, would relate positively with the needs for achievement, autonomy, dominance, and intraception and negatively with the need for succorance, as defined by the

EPPS. Data from 57 female and 12 male college students confirmed only two of the five hypothesized relationships, succorance (-.30) and intraception (.34).

Also interested in activity and passivity and their relationship to perceptual dependence were League and Jackson (1961). Older college males were given a short form of the EFT, an incomplete sentence test of passivity, and a group Rorschach. (In order to measure activity in the Rorschach, subjects were instructed to respond to the entire blot; response measures were total number of responses and total M responses within a given time period.) Subjects also participated in a small group leaderless discussion session in which the number of responses made served as a measure of activity. The only significant correlation obtained between field dependency and activity-passivity was a negative relationship between the total number of Rorschach responses and total EFT time.

Gordon et al (1961) administered to 50 college males the (Gottschaldt) EFT and the Personality Research Inventory, scored for anxiety, frustration tolerance, ambiguity tolerance, self-acceptance, compulsiveness, impulsiveness, and self-sufficiency. Field dependence was found to have correlated with non-self-acceptance and impulsivity. A factor analysis indicated that certain GEFT items are more readily solved by persons characterized by certain personality traits.

Goldstein et al. (1968) administered to 30 hospitalized male alcoholics who scored in the field dependent range on the RFT the following scales: the EPPS (for Deference, Succorance, and Autonomy scale scores), Crowne and Marlowe's Social Desirability Scale, the Guilford-Martin Inventory of Factors (for ascendance and masculinity scale scores), the MMPI (for Pd and Mf scale scores), the Bass Social Acquiescence Scale, Couch and Keniston's Yeasay-Naysay Scale, the Leary Interpersonal Test of Personality (for the Dominance and Love dimensions for both public image and self concept levels), and a measure of intelligence. Correlations between measures of personality and perceptual dependence yielded only two significances and these opposite in direction from that predicted. A factor analysis indicated little commonality between RFT scores and the personality measures and no single factor among the personality measures that could be defined as dependence. In fact, the alcoholics whose RFT scores fell within the field dependent range scored at or below "normal" males on measures of psychological and social dependence where normative data was available. These authors, as a result, questioned the generalizability of perceptual dependence to other definitions of dependence.

Adevai, et al. (1968) administered the MMPI, the Taylor Manifest Anxiety Scale, and the Baron Ego-Strength Scale to 22 field dependent and 22 field independent male and female college students. Perceptual dependence was based on RFT performance. The expected relationships again were not observed. These investigators suggested that personality tests such as the TAT and Rorschach which emphasize the process aspects of personality might be more applicable in determining the relationship between perceptual and psychosocial dependence. It is important to restate that psychological differentiation is a structural aspect rather than a content aspect of a system and that pathological adjustment can be found in persons functioning at any level of differentiation.

Field Dependence and Demographic Factors

Research in the area of perceptual dependence has uncovered certain demographic variables that may be associated with level of differentiation. Among these are sex, age, socioeconomic status, and analytical aspects of intelligence. Existing evidence points to differences in perceptual dependence between males and females, with females displaying lesser degrees of differentiation. Such sex differences are relatively small compared to differences within each sex, but they are persistent and have been observed among persons in late childhood to old age, at which time these differences disappear again. If, indeed, women are more field dependent than men (a condition of which we cannot yet be certain), they may experience much in the way of conflict as they strive for independence in the women's liberation movement. Since the culture has traditionally dictated a more dependent and restricted role for women, such conflict will decrease as the culture changes to make them less perceptually dependent (more differentiated). The following studies suggest origins of sex differences in early parent-child relations.

Sex-role identification. Barclay and Cusumano (1967) compared RFT performance among groups of father-absent and father-present black and white 15-year-old boys. Father absence was defined as absence since age five or younger. The adolescents were administered the Gough Femininity Scale and a semantic differential to determine overt role identification and cross-sex identification. The results showed that father-absent boys were more field dependent than father-present boys; blacks were more perceptually dependent than whites. Interestingly, however, father-absent boys did not differ from father-present boys for masculine identification or for cross-sex identification on an overt level. The authors suggested the possibility of a compensatory adjustment mechanism operating among the father-absent boys. Farr (1969) also reported, among other findings, no relationship between perceptual dependence and sex or sex-role identification among college men and women.

Wohlford and Liberman (1970) compared the performance of father-present and father-absent fourth to sixth grade boys and girls on the Children's EFT. All children were from temporarily broken families whose parents had come to this country from Cuba within the preceding ten years. The median number of months of father absence was 15 months; for half of the father-absent group, absence occurred prior to the child's sixth birthday and for half, after the child's sixth birthday. Father-present children had been without their father for a maximum of one month. As predicted, father-absent children were more field dependent than father-present children; contrary to expectations, however, was the finding that later onset of father absence was associated with the higher degree of field dependence. Because no sex differences were observed for the father-absent group, arguments linking sex typing and perceptual dependence were questioned.

Corah (1965), working with 60 middle- and upper-class children between ages 8 and 11 and their parents, attempted to assess possible relationships between differentiation levels (DL) of children and their parents. He assessed the DL with respect to perceptual and cognitive functions by means of verbal intelligence tests, embedded figures tests and (for the children only) a draw-a-person test. He found that level of differentiation of these children correlated significantly with that of the parent of the opposite sex and not with that of the parent of the same sex.

Lawrence (1969) predicted that females who identify with their father would conform less to the female role model than females who identify with their mother. Of 117 college females, ten who best represented father identifiers and 10 who best represented mother identifiers on the basis of a semantic differential were selected for further study. Results showed that father identifying women tested more field independent (Witkin's Embedded Figures Test); however, other relationships, although generally in the expected direction, proved nonsignificant. Contrary to expectations was the finding that father identifiers were more likely than mother identifiers to have expressed a preference for a housewife-only role as opposed to a career role. In addition, father identifiers were more likely than mother identifiers to have attributed to females the characteristic of aggressiveness; but, overall, both groups reserved the characteristic of dependence for females and the characteristic of aggressiveness for males.

Lynn (1969) proposed a curvilinear relationship between perceptual dependence and identification with the parent of the same sex. Specifically, he suggested that extreme closeness to or distance from the parent of the same sex would inhibit differentiation while moderate closeness or distance would foster greater differentiation. This postulation was based on the availability of appropriate sex-role models with which to identify. Lynn reasoned that for the child who is unusually close to the appropriate parent there would be no or too few additional role models available; thus, the process of identification would become simply one of passive imitation. For the child who is extremely distant from the same-sexed parent, the opportunity to identify with that parent would be either non-existent or, at best, very limited; thus, the sex-role learning would become too difficult for the child. For the moderately distant child, the appropriate model as well as additional sex-role models would be available for identification. Thus, the identification learning would become a more active and complex process, requiring differentiation in terms of thought and feeling processes, and would become available as an instrument for dealing with the world in a more articulated fashion.

The role which cultural factors plays in the differential development of psychological differentiation between sexes has also been considered. Greenwald (1968) obtained a significant correlation between field independent performance on the EFT and preference for an Intellectual Role and a significant correlation between field dependent performance on the EFT and preference for the Woman's Role among subjects given the French and Lesser Student Attitude Scale. Preference for a particular role was said to reflect preference for a certain life style.

Differences in level of differentiation stem from both hereditary and environmental influences. Witkin and his associates (1962) have focused some of their research on the early mother-child relationship and have followed up longitudinally the extent to which and how a mother of a certain level of articulation is able to foster perceptual dependence or independence in her children.

Witkin et al. (1962) presented preliminary evidence that the mother's level of differentiation may indeed influence that of her children. Lapidus (1970) studied activity-passivity and psychological differentiation among 84 pregnant women and related her findings to current social issues. On the basis of interview material, attitude scales, the EFT, and the decision of the women to participate or not in a program preparing them for childbirth, two groups emerged. Those who desired childbirth instruction tested field independent, expressed the wish to breastfeed and personally care for their child, and were opposed to the use of drugs both prior to and during childbirth. The second group, those who did not desire to participate in the childbirth preparation program, scored relatively field dependent, preferred to bottle feed and have another help with infant care, and were not opposed to the use of drugs. Lapidus related indices of active involvement in childbirth to lower infant mortality, less brain injury to the child, and greater success in "planned" pregnancies (population control), and suggested stepping up childbirth preparation programs especially in ghetto areas where learned passivity often becomes a learned life style.

Mother influence on the development of psychological differentiation in her child was also studied by Hauk (1967). With intelligence and socio-economic level controlled, Piaget's conservation test, the Children's EFT, the Reactive Curiosity Scale (broad interest in environment), and 20 items of the Sequential Tests of Educational Progress (STEP) science test were given to 231 fifth and sixth grade boys and girls. Autonomy-control attitudes of mothers were measured by the Parental Attitude Research Inventory (PARI) and a STEP science test to fathers provided data on the cognitive atmosphere of the home. Concept attainment was expected to be less for field dependent, mother-controlled, and less curious children. Among the findings were that mother attitude was not a factor in concept attainment, that curiosity was an important variable only for children whose fathers were non-professionals, and that field dependence was a significant factor in concept attainment only for children whose fathers were professionals.

The interrelationships among siblings has also been considered a factor in articulation development. Winestine (1966) studied perceptual dependence among 30 pairs of identical male twins, 8 to 12 years of age. (Presumably, the hereditary influence is held constant while the environmental factors are variable). It was found that, on the basis of tests of perceptual dependence and interview material dealing with peer and co-twin relationships, twins who tested field dependent evidenced problems in the development of a sense of separate identity.

Stewart (1967) extended the work done by Schacter (1959) and others on birth order and social dependence by examining the correlation between birth order and perceptual dependence. An abbreviated EFT was administered to oldest brothers of brothers, oldest brothers of sisters, youngest brothers of brothers, and youngest brothers of sisters. Subjects were college students. As expected on the basis of previous research, oldest brothers, regardless of the sex of other siblings, performed more field dependently than youngest brothers. Early socialization and parent-child relations may thus provide some clues as to the origin of differences in level of differentiation.

Age. Generally, perceptual dependence has been found to be marked during childhood, to decrease rapidly through adolescence, and to increase during the adult years. (Old age is often accompanied by regression to levels of childlike dependency as well as less differentiated sex role differences.) Schwartz and Karp (1967) investigated field dependence among geriatric patients. In the first study, involving high school students, persons from the community aged 30-39, and geriatric day care patients aged 58-80, perceptual dependence (BAT, RFT, EFT performance) was lower in the high school group, higher in the 30- to 39-year-old group, and highest among the geriatric patients. Sex differences did not occur in the 58- to 80-year-old group. However, the three groups were not comparable: the younger groups were generally middle class, native born, better educated, and still vocationally active; the geriatric group was generally foreign born, poorly educated, and retired.

In another study (Karp, 1967) subjects were all unemployed day center males and females between the ages of 60-92 and divided into three age groups. Perceptual dependence was found to increase with age, but leveled off among 80- to 90-year olds. To test whether this result could be attributed to a developmental plateau or a difference in survival rate among those less perceptually dependent, 20 employed and 20 unemployed males between the ages of 60-75 and divided into two age groups were given the Gottschaldt Embedded Figures Test. The older groups performed more field dependently than the younger groups but the employed group performed more field independently, thus lending support to the selective survival hypothesis. A longitudinal study was in the planning to ascertain the life expectancy of those relatively field independent.

Bloom, et al. (1969) reported that survival may, indeed, be associated with level of psychological differentiation. Infirm aged, diagnosed as "dying" six months after relocation from an old urban facility to a modern suburban one, tended to score more field dependently on the Children's EFT (a modified scoring procedure was used) than those diagnosed as "surviving." "With his clearer sense of self and body, the field independent person maintains an underlying unity which persists despite change in physical environment or social context." In other words, he is less dependent on external frames of reference for self-definition.

The increase of perceptual dependency with age and its observed relationship to actual dependency in the life space of the individual has important implications in the rehabilitation of the geriatric patient. It is essential that the elderly patient be given opportunities for independent functioning-both in terms of his own self care and activities to occupy his leisure time. However, it should be recognized that procedures which drastically change the perceptual field upon which he is dependent can increase anxiety or cause the patient's withdrawal from interaction with his environment. Expressed in other terms, the geriatric patient must be provided with activities which give him an opportunity for ego involvement in a way which assists in the maintenance of his identity (a process which society at large in its disengagement philosophy denies the elderly individual). Such identity maintenance may act as a counter force to the increase of field dependency with age.

Socioeconomic factors. Because of differences in experience (both quantitative and qualitative) which can serve to function as facilitators or inhibitors of psychological differentiation, one might expect differences in levels of perceptual dependence between rural and urban dwellers and among the various socio-economic classes.

Reppen (1967) investigated the effect of socio-economic status and rural-urban residence on perceptual dependency. These variables were then related to measures of personal and social adjustment, intelligence, and sex. The subjects were nearly 300 sixth grade boys and girls divided into 12 groups representing the various sex, class, and rural-urban combinations. It was predicted that, because a rural environment might be considered relatively lacking in stimuli, children from these areas would suffer from inadequate stimulus exposure and thus their potential for differentiation would be less. The results supported the hypothesis: the rural group performed more field dependently than the urban group. It was also determined that girls performed more field dependently than boys, and that the lower the socio-economic status, the greater the perceptual dependence.

Karp, et al. (1969) predicted that socio-economic status would not be a factor in field articulation. They gave lower class black and middle class white adolescent boys the EFT, draw-a-person test, and 3 verbal and 3 performance subtests of the WISC. Although the two groups did not differ significantly on the EFT and draw-a-person test, the middle-class boys performed significantly better on the Block Design subtest, which has been shown to correlate highly with field dependency. In a second study the influence of factors associated with race was eliminated. Karp, et al. compared EFT performance of 40-year-old middle and lower class white males (as differentiated by the Index of Social Position). EFT performance did not reflect class differences.

Intelligence. Dubois and Cohen (1970) questioned the assumption that field independence-dependence is related only to those measures of intelligence requiring the same analytical abilities, i.e., overcoming embedded contexts. The EFT and RFT were individually administered to 143 undergraduate females, with scores from the (New York) State University Admissions Examination (SUAE) obtained previously. The ten SUAE scores (verbal aptitude, quantitative aptitude, total aptitude, achievement in five academic areas, total achievement, and total aptitude and achievement) were correlated with both EFT and RFT performance. Low but statistically significant correlations were obtained for all RFT-SUAE scores and 8 out of 10 EFT-SUAE scores. The authors concluded that it may be premature to discount the role that general (verbal and nonverbal) intelligence plays in field independent-dependent performance.

Stability of field dependence. Although most studies have shown field dependence-independence to be relatively stable over time and unaffected by experimental treatment, Goldstein and Chotlas (1966) found that RFT performance improved for a group of 62 male alcoholics following an 8-10 week period of abstinence due to participation in an inpatient treatment program. However, a comparable study by Jacobson (1970) et al. supported the stability hypothesis. The RFT was administered to 37 male alcoholics approximately 10 days after admission to a hospital treatment unit and again a day or two prior to discharge. The mean number of days between testing was 33. Test-retest performance did not differ significantly. Changes in internal and external sensory environment (abstinence and hospitalization) had no effect on level of perceptual dependence.

Jacobson (1966, 1968) demonstrated significant reductions in field dependence following 1-hour stimulus deprivation among male college students and alcohol dependents using pre- and post-test RFTs. Astrup (1968) showed not only that short-term stimulus deprivation can result in reduced perceptual dependency but also that long-term deprivation could actually stabilize the "shift" toward field independence. Astrup gave the RFT to two groups of student miners in South Africa before and after a day shift underground. One group had been underground for six months; the other, two weeks. The six-month group performed significantly more field independently on the pretest RFT than did the two-week group. In addition, the six-month group showed no change on retest (stable) whereas the two-week group performed more field independently than they did prior to a shift underground. The results of these studies can be "explained on the basis of increased awareness of bodily sensations and their availability for use in orientation tasks."

That mode of perceptual dependence be viewed as a relatively stable, unalterable, habitual way of responding was also questioned by Rudin (1968). He postulated instead that perceptual mode was a matter of preference rather than ability and, therefore, subject to change as a function of motivation. The RFT, the Self Contextual Influence Test (SCI), and the Role Contextual Influence Test (RCI), were administered to college males. The SCI requires that the subject imagine himself in each of four situations and describe himself on rating scales; the RCI is similar but the subject is required to play a role. According to the differentiation hypothesis, field dependent subjects are expected to rate themselves differently from one situation to the next, thus allowing the situation to influence their feelings. Prior to test administration, Rudin instructed the students in one instance to allow the situation to influence their feelings and in another to ignore the situation. The results supported his hypothesis and the broader concept of ego autonomy (a kind of perceptual flexibility) was suggested. Subjects who were able to shift as a function of instructional set tested less perceptually dependent.

Rudin's hypothesis raises an interesting possibility in the area of technique for the rehabilitation counselor. Perhaps the counselor might try to decrease the client's dependence upon the field by using his legitimate authority and relationship with the client to suggest that he be less affected and influenced by other people and more expressive of goals and ideas which are syntonic to his own needs and feelings. In other words, the process would involve encouraging the client to say and do what he feels is best for him rather than what will be most accepted by the individuals in his life who comprise his interpersonal field.

Field Dependence and External vs. Internal Orientation

Witkin, et al. (1962) suggested that perceptually independent persons are idea-oriented while those perceptually dependent are people-oriented. On the basis of EFT scores, Brilhart (1966) selected male engineering students who scored highly field dependent, moderately field dependent, and highly field independent and had them listen to a speech of a persuasive nature under one of two speaker message conditions: (1) presentation good, argument poor; (2) presentation poor, argument good. Afterward, the students filled out various forms from which indices of speaker-message criticism and attitude shift were obtained. The expected positive association between greater field independence and lower speaker-higher message criticisms was partially supported. However, level of perceptual dependence was not associated with attitude change as a function of speaker-message quality. Further support for the hypothesized relationship between field dependence and relative orientation toward people and field independence and relative orientation toward aspects of the environment other than people was again obtained by Brilhart (1970).

Gary (1968) presented fictitious biographical and research abstracts to 60 subjects who then rated the unpaired author-research abstracts for confidence in author expertise and correctness of research conclusions. At a subsequent time subjects rerated the paired author-research abstracts (paired by the experimenter in terms of similar and dissimilar subject ratings, e.g. high-high, high-low, low-high, and low-low author-abstract confidence levels). Subjects were also given the EFT. Among other findings, perceptually dependent subjects did not assign higher ratings for the high author-low abstract pairs nor did the perceptually independent subjects assign higher ratings for the low author-high abstracts pairs. Neither did the perceptual dependents differ from the perceptual independents in terms of changed ratings.

DiStefano (1970) extended the differentiation hypothesis to include interpersonal perception. Five extremely field independent and five extremely field dependent male high school teachers and 110 of their male students took the EFT; teachers and students described one another on semantic differential and other scales. The major finding, that students and teachers scoring similarly held positive attitudes and feelings toward one another while those scoring dissimilarly held negative attitudes and feelings, might have implications for client-counselor situation. This finding presents a rather intriguing possibility for the rehabilitation of exceedingly difficult clients. In these cases clients could be administered the EFT and be assigned to counselors with known similar EFT scores. In this way the probability of gaining a more effective treatment relationship more quickly might be enhanced.

Other studies have dealt with the relationship between perceptual dependence and reliance upon external frames of reference for guidance or support. Because field dependents tend to rely upon others for approval and support, Messick and Damarin (1964) hypothesized that they, relative to field independents, would be more attentive to facial features and expressions and would, therefore, be better able to recall faces previously exposed to. Ten female and 40 male college students were given the Hidden Figures Test and asked to estimate the age of 79 persons whose faces were photographed without the knowledge that they would subsequently be called upon to estimate the age of an additional 40 persons and to identify those faces which had previously been seen on the initial photograph presentation. The hypothesis was confirmed, demonstrating the importance of other people in satisfying the strong social needs of field dependents. Thus, we stress the importance of the counselor's awareness of the field dependent client's sensitivity to cues of the counselor (verbal and nonverbal) which indicate changes in his attitude and general climate of the treatment situation. In addition, if the client tests field dependent, his participation as part of an accepting social group could be most helpful to rehabilitation progress.

Further evidence of field dependent persons' need for and reliance upon others for approval and support comes from a study by Konstadt and Forman (1965). Selected from 90 fourth-grade boys and girls were 38 children who scored at the extremes on the Children's EFT. Subjects were twice given the Letter Cancellation Test (a routine paper-and-pencil task), once by an experimenter who verbally reinforced performance and once by an experimenter who verbally punished performance. In terms of task performance, field dependent groups did not differ except under the disapproval condition where the field dependent children performed significantly poorer. In terms of attention to others in the room, field dependent children looked to others significantly more often than did field independent children during disapproval and most often when approval preceded disapproval. Thus, whether a structural-developmental or a content-motivational approach to dependency is employed, performance of dependent persons suffers substantially when they have been socially deprived.

On the basis of the group EFT and the Sophistication-of-Body Concept Scale, Carrigan (1967) selected 30 field dependent and 30 field independent college students and subjected half from each group to physical stress (cold pressor test) and the other half to psychological stress (criticism). Perceptually dependent subjects coped with the criticism through dependence on the experimenter whereas perceptually independent subjects relied upon their own resources in handling the situation. Deever (1968) found that college students who test field dependent on the EFT and externally-oriented on the Social Reaction Inventory based their expected performance levels (on a laboratory task) on the levels achieved by others before them whereas those who tested field independent and internally oriented based their expected performance levels on their own past performance levels.

Another study which focused on the use of internal vs. external frames of reference was one carried out by Barr (1968) using college males. The tendency to conform (in an Asch-type situation, on a measure of attitude change and on a test of reasoning) was found to be positively associated with two measures of perceptual dependence. Clark (1968) demonstrated the relationship between perceptual dependence and authoritarianism. Based on a measure of authoritarian attitudes, 20 subjects whose scores fell at each extreme of the distribution were given the EFT and the School and College Ability Test (SCAT). High authoritarianism was associated with field dependence and lower total and verbal SCAT scores.

The Higgen Figures Test (HFT) and the Adult's Locus of Evaluation and Control Scale (ALOE-C) were administered by Willoughby (1967) to 76 male and female college students. The ALOE-C measures the extent to which a person depends upon an outside source for self-evaluation and the extent to which he perceives himself as in control of his environment. As expected, reliance upon an external frame of reference was positively related to perceptual dependence while perception of self as the controlling agent was unrelated. No relationship between sex and field dependence was observed.

That diffusion of responsibility increases the amount of risk taking among perceptually dependent persons was demonstrated by Wallach, et al. (1967). Over 600 male and female college students were given the EFT and the Choice Dilemmas procedure, a measure of risk taking. Subjects who scored in the moderately field dependent third of the EFT distribution were eliminated. Although all subjects were more willing to take risks after small group discussion sessions, perceptually dependent subjects were more often shifted toward a more risky position while the perceptually independent subjects more often shifted toward a more conservative position or did not change at all after longer periods of group influence. Furthermore, field dependent subjects but not field independent subjects judged the group over themselves as responsible for larger shifts toward a more risky position.

The level of field dependency of the rehabilitation client may well provide the practitioner with a clue to his initial treatment approach. With an individual who shows high dependence upon his field of perception a more directive or manipulative technique could motivate the patient until he can be encouraged to more effectively act under his own motivational power. The client who is relatively field independent may require a less directive approach on the part of the rehabilitation practitioner and respond best to an allowance of greater degrees of self determination.

Thus far, we have concerned ourselves with various aspects and ramifications of perceptual dependency. Some of these knowledge segments merit further exploration for application to the field of rehabilitation. The material which follows, however, links perceptual dependency to treatment, a central procedure in the rehabilitation process.

Field Dependence, Treatment, Placement

Whitehorn and Betz (1960) observed that physicians differed in their relationships with patients and that these differences correlated with vocational interest patterns. Specifically, when therapists were directive or passive observing they tended to show interest in vocations requiring preciseness and a mechanistic approach. In contrast, therapists who formed personal and mutual relationships with their clients tended to prefer vocations requiring flexibility in thought and approach.

Based on these findings, Pollack and Kiev (1963) postulated that therapists who interacted more extensively with their patients and preferred vocations requiring flexibility would perform neither perceptually dependent nor perceptually independent on the RFT. On the other hand, therapists who preferred employing a directive approach with clients and vocations that demanded adherence to procedure and scientific principles were expected to perform perceptually independent. Further, therapists who preferred a passive observing approach with clients and vocations that required preciseness were expected to perform perceptually dependent on the RFT. Subjects were 40 male therapists from a psychiatric clinic. Vocational interest was measured by the Strong Vocational Interest Blank. The results confirmed the hypothesis with the exception that there was no difference on the RFT between therapists who used directive and passive observing counseling styles. These therapists, who maintained a more detached relationship, performed perceptually independent on the RFT. The absence of field dependent therapists might be explained in terms of their choice of profession and the kinds of analytical abilities it requires. Further support of these findings was obtained by Shows and Carson (1965) using nonprofessional male students and a shortened form of the Strong.

That therapists of differing cognitive styles evidence differential success rates with different types of persons has been illustrated (Whitehorn and Betz, 1960; McNair et al. 1962). Goodman and Buchheimer (1966) suggested that structural (i.e., interaction with client) as opposed to content aspects be stressed as an integral part of the counselor training process. They observed counselors-in-training responding in the presence of a supervisor to video tapes of actual counseling situations to which the real counselor's responses were omitted. Highly articulated counselors were described as ". . . able to express spontaneous feelings about the counselee; spontaneously developed and revised their counseling leads as a result of their reformulation of counselee problems; and maintained an active and task-oriented approach to the film exercise." Counselors who were field dependent, on the other hand, were "unable to break a set provided by the counselee's statements when other reactions were occurring; could not make use of counselee emotional reactions as sources of information; would get annoyed with the counselee when he expressed socially unacceptable wishes; and had difficulty developing or revising their counseling leads. . . . Expressions of helplessness, unquestioning acceptance of supervisor statements, and an anxious driven talkativeness was exhibited by low field articulators."

"In therapy, persons functioning at a more or less differentiated level are likely to differ in presenting symptoms, suitability for psychotherapy, nature of relation to therapist (transference), and prospects for change" (Witkin, 1965). The first attempt to study the kinds of things that occur within the counseling situation as a function of patient and therapist level of differentiation was made by Witkin et al. (1968). Investigated were certain patient-expressed feelings and patient-therapist interactions at an outpatient clinic during early psychotherapy sessions. Each of four counselors was assigned one field dependent and one field independent patient. Transcribed tapes were then scored for direct and indirect patient-expressed feelings of anxiety and hostility in terms of both intensity of feeling and frequency of spurts of these feelings as well as patient-therapist interactions in terms of number of therapist comments and number of words and time per patient response (tempo). As predicted, field independent patients expressed more guilt (aroused by specific violations of one's own standards of behavior) than shame anxiety (aroused by perceived violations of someone else's standards of behavior), more outward-directed hostility (less fear of separation from therapist) than inward-directed anxiety, and less diffuse anxiety (in which the source is vague or nonspecific). Further, sessions with field independent patients were characterized by longer intervals between patient-therapist remarks (field independent persons tend to consider information in terms of their own established frames of reference) and by a slower therapy tempo.

Therapists, tested for level of differentiation subsequent to the therapy sessions, also showed certain tendencies. Generally, the greater the level of differentiation among therapists, the less the therapist intervened and the slower the session tempo. Finally, in looking at patient-therapist combinations in terms of level of differentiation, the ranking from high to low in terms of frequency of interaction and tempo was as follows: both patient and therapist relatively field dependent; patient field dependent, therapist field independent; patient field independent, therapist field dependent; both patient and therapist field independent.

Witkin et al. stated that "These observations together suggest the usefulness of a study in which therapists selected for extent of differentiation are paired with patients also selected on the basis of level of differentiation." This might well prove a fruitful area of research for the field of rehabilitation.

Further evidence supporting the relevance of field dependence as a subject variable in therapy selection and as a predictor of therapy completion was reported by Karp et al. (1970). Comparisons were made among alcoholics assigned to individual "insight" therapy, alcoholics not selected for insight therapy, and alcoholics assigned to drug therapy. Assignment was based upon psychological evaluation procedures. All subjects were given the short form of the EFT. In addition, groups were divided into "remainers" and "dropouts" on the basis of median number of therapy visits. The findings showed that alcoholics evaluated as able to benefit from insight therapy (in which the patient is required to actively participate in analyzing his own feelings and behavior) performed more field independently than either those not selected for insight therapy or those selected for drug therapy (in which the patient is required to be no more than a passive recipient of the drug regimen). Although the EFT did not differentiate the dropouts from the remainers when all subjects were pooled, dropouts from insight therapy (but not from drug therapy) performed more field dependently than remainers. Speculations were offered regarding the absence of an expected difference in field dependence between dropouts and remainers in drug therapy.

Reimer (1968) attempted to determine the relative effectiveness of kinds of reward and task for college males characterized by different levels of psychological differentiation (Hidden Figures Test) and need for social approval (Marlowe-Crowne Social Desirability Scale). It was predicted that approval reinforcement and verbal conditioning would be more appropriate for field dependents while field independents would perform better under appraisal reinforcement and problem solving conditions. Field dependent subjects were found to be significantly more responsive to approval reinforcement than were field independents; other results concerning perceptual dependence were less conclusive. Possibly then, if a rehabilitation practitioner has field dependence data on a client, he will be better able to determine whether his attitudes should be approving or evaluative in order to best motivate the client.

The following two studies have implications for vocational planning and placement. Because certain occupations require more in terms of analytical ability than others, it would seem reasonable to assume that persons holding positions within such fields would be more field independent than persons who never sought or who failed to achieve such positions. Barrett and Thornton (1967) compared male engineers and technicians in engineering to nondegreed college students who were comparable to Witkin's standardization sample. Although field independence has been shown to decrease somewhat with age, the engineers tested significantly more field independent on the RFT than the younger college students. Other factors such as intelligence and the effects of adult role responsibility were discussed but these could not account for the exceptionally highly developed perceptual capacities displayed by the engineers. Rehabilitation practitioners may wish to consider perceptual dependence-independence, in addition to the standard tests of occupational aptitudes and interests, in vocational planning for their clients.

Gruenfeld and Weissenburg (1970) postulated that sources of job satisfaction and dissatisfaction would be related to the perceiver's level of field independence-dependence. Specifically, field dependents, less able to differentiate between themselves and the environment and more attuned to social aspects of their environment, were expected to choose both intrinsic (e.g. work itself, recognition, responsibility) and extrinsic (e.g. interpersonal relations, working conditions, salary) job factors as satisfiers or dissatisfiers. Field independents, on the other hand, less attuned to their social environment and more interested in mastering their environment, were expected to choose intrinsic job factors as satisfiers or dissatisfiers. The Group EFT and a job satisfaction questionnaire were administered to 96 male state civil service supervisors as well as an item designed to tap their overall job satisfaction. Both hypotheses were supported. The rehabilitation counselor may wish to consider client placement in light of the kinds of job rewards and client level of articulation.

In concluding this section it is important to reemphasize that level of perceptual dependence of the counselor may profoundly influence his technique and indeed his success with a given rehabilitation client. Exactly what this influence may be must be determined through further study. However, overidentification with or rejection of the client by the counselor with perceptual dependence level like or unlike his own may be a possibility. However, the constantly sought self awareness by the counselor may be in his knowledge of his own perceptual dependency. The idea certainly merits further systematized research.

Implications for Rehabilitation

The literature indicates that possible implications of research on perceptual dependency have not been adequately considered by rehabilitation professionals. Yet, the possible value of experimentation with the application of perceptual dependency theory to rehabilitation practice could be highly significant in certain areas. We would suggest that further perceptual dependency research be done along the following dimensions:

1. Rehabilitation Counselor-Client Matching
Rehabilitation clients relate differently to differing personality configurations in counselors. In this regard, perhaps when both client and counselor are similar in their level of perceptual (field) dependency, they may develop greater empathy. On the other hand, opposite polarity along the perceptual dependency dimension may produce an attraction which builds the counselor-client relationship. If the level of field dependency in the personality of the participants in the rehabilitation relationship influences its course, then advance knowledge of the degree of field dependency could become an important factor in counselor-case assignment. Witkin et al. (1968) have already initiated work in this area.

2. Style of Counseling
During the past two decades there has been much discussion concerning the relative merits of directive and nondirective counseling. While it is now generally conceded that both styles have their place in appropriate counseling situations, it has been hypothesized that some personalities respond more successfully to a counseling style which sometimes mixes and sometimes emphasizes particular approaches. Perhaps, the level of perceptual dependency in the client influences his responses to the rehabilitation counselor's style. The authors would recommend further testing of the hypothesis that clients who are field dependent would respond best to a more directive style of rehabilitation counseling. Were this hypothesis to be confirmed, then the rehabilitation counseling procedure could become somewhat more objective, more teachable and less dependent upon hunch and counselor intuition. In addition, counselors who are less field dependent may be more directive in their approach to clients. Thus, the concept of field dependency when more completely researched in regard to its application to the counseling process could not only provide a vehicle which might aid counselor training and supervision (Goodman & Buccheimer, 1966)... but if adequately developed might offer one important criterion for the selection of candidates who are contemplating entry into the field of rehabilitation counseling. Because tests of field dependency are available, research in this area can be considered feasible.

3. Job Placement
A third implication of the perceptual dependency concept in rehabilitation lies

in its possible value as an aid in job selection for the handicapped client. It can be assumed that there are probably some jobs which require more perceptual independence than others while some vocational placements require a fairly good balance between field dependence and independence. Thus, there might be a greater probability of adequate vocational success for rehabilitation clients who are helped to select and train for jobs which have perceptual dependency requirements that are congruent with their perceptual dependency characteristics. At this point little is known concerning the relationship of perceptual dependency to job performance. Such knowledge could be important to job evaluators.

4. Modification of Perceptual Style

A major implication for the field of rehabilitation lies in the highly speculative question of whether or not perceptual dependency itself can be modified or changed and maintained. The relationship between an individual's perceptual dependence and his psychosocial dependence upon his immediate environment could be important. If by lowering a handicapped person's perceptual dependence or increasing his level of differentiation we could lower the individual's over-dependence upon this immediate environment, rehabilitation could advance more quickly and effectively.

5

Rehabilitation of the Dependent Client

In no field are the problems and concepts of dependency more important than in the field of rehabilitation. In a sense, the reduction of the client's instrumental dependency is rehabilitation's reason for being. For the professional practitioner of rehabilitation, the management of dependency is both goal and process. Switzer (1963) highlighted rehabilitation as a major deterrent to dependency and cited the public's financial support of rehabilitation programs as evidence of the recognition of this idea.

Dependency in the Handicapped

During the past twenty years the field of rehabilitation has made significant contributions to the problems involved in coping with the dependency problems of the physically and mentally handicapped. Perhaps most significant was the recognition that dependency is not always disadvantageous and in certain situations is actually functional for the client. According to Coburn (1963) American society has unrealistically overstressed the value of independence, attributing weakness to dependent behavior. The disabled person, realistically dependent, is consequently led to feel useless, dejected, and rejected. It was postulated that, when untempered by dependence, independence is actually an unsound societal value characterized by pathology and ruthlessness.

Havens (1963) also stressed the usefulness of dependency by pointing out that all people are involved in a large network of dependent relationships. Moreover, he takes the position that it is the distribution rather than the amount of dependence which is the critical factor. Dependency spread among a number of relationships should not be considered unhealthy. On the other hand, dependency concentrated within a few relationships (with one or very few people) can be pathological and destructive. Havens stressed the point that without dependence there can be no treatment relationship during which the client can be weaned toward independence. In making his thesis that all dependency cannot be categorically classified as bad, Havens remarked:

Before accusing too many people of being in this dependent condition, for example those on welfare rolls, it is well to look over the individual situation carefully. Some of us look dependent for periods because we are 'resting.' Vacations are such dependent intervals. In another instance we may be dependent in one sphere of our lives because we are putting out more than we are getting back elsewhere. . . . Some of our clients are bearing burdens that make their dependence on us an understandable act of balance. There is in such cases no lack of reciprocity, but we are not the ones reciprocated.

Research findings have indicated that dependency is an important correlate of various types of physical and mental illness. If rehabilitation is to proceed successfully, it is imperative for the counselor and other professionals who work with the client to understand the dependency factor as it relates to the particular handicap being rehabilitated.

Physical Disability

Apart from the reality-based dependency arising from illness, other dependencies are frequently concurrent with the primary dependency. Ludwig and Collette (1970) demonstrated that in addition to the physical limitations imposed by disability, the social isolation and economic and personal care dependencies which often accompany disability contribute also to the patient's mental health status. Subjects, 1965 applicants for Social Security benefits, were interviewed with respect to degree of physical limitation (physical mobility), degree of dependency (personal care activities and source and amount of personal income), and degree of social isolation (social contact with others on a visiting basis); in addition, a short mental health questionnaire was administered. Poorer mental health was associated with each of the three dependent variables; adverse effects were not notable when restricted mobility was viewed in combination with social isolation and with dependency. Mental health was better among those whose normal role functioning was least disrupted and most socially acceptable e.g., over age 65, income from retirement source, etc.

For adult patients who become severely disabled, such as paraplegics described by Meyer (1964), tremendous physical dependency is often accompanied by feelings of dependency reminiscent of those in early childhood. Such feelings lead to conflict over dependency. When patients have a history of successful social functioning they can look to their past adjustment patterns and achievements as models for adjusting to this new life crisis. As part of this, they attribute to individual members of the rehabilitation staff qualities of important figures in their early lives (e.g. mothering, supporting, teaching) which helped them to move from their childhood dependency to adult functioning. As the patient moves into each new area he has a feeling of helplessness. It is this feeling that the patient must accept before he can achieve maximum rehabilitation. The patient who denies the need for help from others often impedes his progress from dependence to independence. The cycle may be likened to that of the adolescent as he struggles to achieve the independence of adulthood. By allowing for the "reenactment" of earlier experiences the rehabilitation milieu permits the disabled to move gradually from regression to a resolution of the dependency-independency conflict.

The problem of dependence in persons with orthopedic and neuromuscular handicaps is compounded by the fact that the handicap is highly visible and produces a change in the client's perception of his body image. In some patients this visibility causes a reaction formation such that they are unable to accept their dependent needs. Other individuals so handicapped become extremely dependent because their dependence is so obviously justified. There are also status problems which develop. Since the person feels different and inferior in social status, he may compensate for these feelings of inferiority by becoming highly dependent and demanding. The orthopedic neuromuscular handicap drastically influences the person's self concept.

Wright (1960) pointed out that:

The kind of person you think you are becomes endowed with remarkable powers. It influences, and often decisively, the way one perceives the intention of others, the choice of associates, the goal set for oneself and much more. The self concept, then, is an important part of one's world of life space and has been so recognized by our eminent psychological forefathers who have given serious attention to its development.

There can be little doubt that the self-concept of the orthopedic-neuromuscular handicapped individual profoundly influences and shapes the character of his dependent strivings.

The particular emotional climate which pervades the handicapped individual's life-space is of great consequence in determining how he deals with his own dependent strivings and whether or not he becomes successfully rehabilitated. Krause (1962) studied a group of blind clients undergoing rehabilitation at a center to determine the effects of dependence on their family setting upon progress in the rehabilitation program. Preliminary research findings indicated that clients living away from home during the rehabilitation process made greater gains from the therapeutic work milieu than those who lived with their own family. Case studies showed that once they returned home the blind clients relapsed into earlier patterns of dependency upon their families. Krause suggested that supportive casework with the families of the blind rehabilitees may speed up the progress of blind persons living at home during training for work.

In studying dependency in the blind, Green (1966) distinguished between instrumental and emotional dependence. Instrumental dependence referred to that behavior which can elicit from others the means by which overt needs can be satisfied (measured by help requested on an auditory task); emotional dependence referred to that behavior which can elicit from others direct satisfaction of covert needs (measured by the Rhodes Sentence Completion Test). It was predicted that both instrumental and emotional dependence would be higher for the blind than for the sighted and would increase as length of time blind increased. The subjects were 56 permanently and totally blind males and 14 sighted between the ages of 20 and 54. The blind were divided into four groups on the basis of length of time blind (range was 4 months to 11 years). As predicted both instrumental and emotional dependence were higher for the blind than for the sighted. Instrumental dependence increased with time blind, indicating that the blind probably learned that the most expeditious way of achieving goals was to depend upon others for help. Contrary to expectations, emotional dependence decreased as time blind increased; it was suggested that the blind may have with time, developed the mechanisms necessary to cope with their blindness.

Swift et al. (1967) compared a group of 50 diabetic boys and girls in early adolescence to a well matched group of 50 nondiabetics on various adjustment variables, one of which was dependency. On the basis of clinical evaluations and Rorschach material, diabetics were shown to be significantly more dependent and conflicted over dependency than their controls (it was pointed out that dependency may be characteristic of any chronic illness, not diabetes per se). Further, highly dependent or overly defensive independent diabetics were medically evaluated as evidencing less adequate control over their disease than were diabetics whose dependent-independent functioning was less extreme. Because of the interrelationships that were obtained among dependency, poorer self image (House-Tree-Person test) and poorer disease control, the authors suggested that the diabetic youngster be given responsibility for disease regulation as soon as is feasible in order to both prevent dependency upon others and to foster a sense of competence and worth.

Goodman (1964) found that adolescents who are communication-impaired show somewhat greater social immaturity than their noncommunication-impaired counterparts. It was suggested that the immaturity results from their greater dependency on others due to difficulties in communicating their needs, understanding, and being understood. Similarly, in a study of 203 epileptic adolescents Goldin et al. (1971) found in a number of subjects social maturity problems which were apparently related to overprotective behavior on the part of parents.

Dependency is frequently exhibited by the cardiovascular patient. In a study of a single case, Meinhardt and Robinson (1962) observed that intense emotion arising from ungratified dependency needs was primarily responsible for the occurrence of a complete heart block. Rehabilitation counseling with the cardiac patient is particularly difficult because his concern with his limitations has some basis in reality. Moreover, the cardiac patient poses a difficult problem with respect to his own dependency conflict because of the invisibility of his handicap. Except in cases of stroke, where there is visible motor impairment, the cardiac patient appears no different from one with a normal cardiovascular system. Thus, he feels that others cannot always go about justifying his dependent behavior; he may develop conflict between his need to show independent behavior and his own dependency strivings.

The invisibility of the cardiac patient's handicap poses a number of problems. In some instances it is necessary for the counselor to help his client accept his feelings of dependency rather than to compensate for them. Also, it is important that the cardiac patient is placed in a position which will bolster his feelings of adequacy so that he does not feel that his dependency requires explanation.

The unique dependency problem confronting the organ transplant patient during postoperative adjustment was described by Crammond (1967). Kidney transplant donors and recipients were interviewed prior to and following surgery in order to evaluate personality functioning. Four of five cases presented illustrated strong ambivalent feelings on the part of the recipient toward his donor. On the one hand, the recipient is grateful to the donor for giving him a new lease on life but, on the other, resents not being able to do anything for the donor in return. In order to alleviate his guilt feelings, the recipient often attempts to do something very special with his life in lieu of payment. The donor, for his part, behaves very protectively toward the recipient which further exacerbates the recipient's feelings of guilt. Crammond recommended that psychological evaluation be considered an important criterion for donor selection. Heightened postoperative levels of dependency in basically dependent persons will further complicate rehabilitation efforts.

Emotional Disorders

There is little evidence to suggest that the problems of client dependency are more difficult in rehabilitating persons with one type of handicap than another. There is a wide range of differences in individuals which affect the course of rehabilitation but which are not directly related to type of handicap. Moreover, all types of handicaps have special problems which cause difficulty.

Yet, because of the long standing public stigma attached to it, mental illness creates dependency problems for the patient which block his rehabilitation and taxes the skill of the rehabilitation counselor to its utmost. This is not a pessimistic point of view. The mental patient can be effectively rehabilitated but the dependency problems are great. To attain any measure of independence, the patient must deal with and overcome strong leanings toward dependence which are conditioned by his sheltered existence within the mental hospital. Moreover, he must face the risk of ridicule, misunderstanding, and discrimination by a large segment of the community. Couple these problems with the fact that many mental patients had high dependency components within their personality structure prior to their illness and the true magnitude of the dependency problem becomes starkly evident.

Studies of mental patients by Freeman and Simmons (1965) showed findings similar to those of Krause in that patients who lived with their spouses were more independent and became rehabilitated more quickly than those living with their parents.

Robbins (1969) reviewed the literature on the psychosomatic origins of neurodermatitis, essential hypertension, arthritis, asthma, and peptic ulcers. Although the latter two illnesses have traditionally been thought to have origins in unmet or frustrated dependency needs, evidence supporting the dependency as cause component of asthma appears to be less conclusive than that for ulcers. The author pointed out that most psychosomatic research has focused on dependency and hostility to the exclusion of other personality factors and thus the relationship between psychosomatic illness and personality is far from complete.

Speisman and Singer (1961) found that an ulcer group produced significantly more dependency responses to Rorschach cards than did other groups with organic pathology. Weiss and Emmerich (1962) compared three groups—ulcer, non-ulcer psychosomatic, and non-psychosomatic—as to need for dependence on TAT stories and need to conform in an Asch-type situation. Both the ulcer and psychosomatic groups revealed significantly greater dependency needs than did the nonpsychosomatic group. Significantly higher conformity needs were observed for the non-psychosomatic group over those of the ulcer and nonulcer psychosomatic groups. Other inter-group comparisons were not significant.

Marshall (1960) administered the EPPS and the Peptic Ulcer Index (a self and ideal self rating scale dealing with the variables of dominance, aggression, efficiency, responsibility, self-sufficiency, strict moralism, emotional inhibition and conformity) to groups of 40 ulcer, 20 psychosomatic nongastrointestinal and 20 nonpsychosomatic patients, all hospitalized Army soldiers on active duty. Since the non-ulcer groups did not differ significantly on the variable under consideration they were combined for the purpose of analysis. Results indicated that the ulcer group was significantly more conforming and more emotionally inhibited than the non-ulcer group; other differences were not significant. Moreover, there were no differences in dependency conflict among groups as measured by the discrepancy scores between the self and ideal self ratings. Only intraception on the EPPS differentiated the groups—ulcer patients scored significantly lower than did the non-ulcer patients; no differences between groups occurred on the achievement, change, dominance, and aggression scales.

Zola (1967) studied the effect of separation from parents on the dependency behavior of hospitalized asthmatics and respiratory patients and nonhospitalized controls. Subjects were 33 5- 11-year old boys. The TAT was used to assess dependency both at the time of hospitalization and again six months later at home. It was predicted that asthmatics would display a greater need for dependence in general and a greater increase in need for dependence accompanying separation than would nonasthmatics. Results showed that dependency scores were higher for asthmatics but only during separation from their parents.

As predicted, need for dependence increased during separation relative to that for nonasthmatics; this finding was discussed in terms of the asthmatic's conflict over his dependency needs, the defenses erected to guard against expressions of dependency and the subsequent breakdown of the defenses under stress conditions.

Stuttering has been long regarded as symptomatic of underlying unmet dependency needs. Sadoff and Collins (1968) described the passive-dependent personality characteristics of 20 of 22 stutterers undergoing group psychotherapy and the ways in which the stuttering itself serves to satisfy dependency strivings. They suggested that, prior to attempts to reduce the stuttering, the helping professional concentrate on identifying the need satisfactions obtained by stuttering and help the patient accept these needs and the role they play in symptom maintenance.

Also interpreted as symptomatic of deep-seated dependency needs were trichotillomania or hair-pulling symbiosis (Greenberg, 1969), gingival mutilation, nontalking (sometimes referred to as elective mutism), regional enteritis, and school phobia. Hoffman and Baer (1968) presented three cases involving self-imposed gingival lesions, illustrating the regressive manner by which these children sought and obtained dependency gratification from their parents. Wright (1968) described the refusal of 24 children to talk outside of the home and attributed this behavior largely to the mother-child relationship which contained elements of dependence, ambivalence, and a need to control. A short-term treatment approach was offered and follow-up data indicated a generally favorable prognosis. On the basis of psychiatric evaluations, Ford et al. (1969) characterized nearly two thirds of young adult patients suffering from regional enteritis as dependent or in conflict over their need to depend on others. Like their parents, enteritis patients showed a high incidence of obessive-compulsive and hypochondriacal traits and inhibition in interpersonal relations. Enteritis attacks often appeared to be precipitated by stress within the home and served to preserve dependency relationships with family members. Finally, Berg et al. (1969) administered to mothers of 29 school phobic adolescents a questionnaire concerning their child's dependency and found a high degree of mother-child attachment and greater orientation of the child toward the family and home environment than toward his peer group.

Buskirk et al. (1968) noted among emotionally disturbed children an overwhelming anxiety accompanying separation situations and suggested that its roots might lie in earlier but unsuccessful attempts to resolve the dependency conflict inherent in the developmental task of separation from the mother. The children were described as having achieved an autonomy which was egocentric, rather than social, in nature and which functioned as a defense against fears surrounding dependency relationships with others. Ways in which occupational therapists can help such children resolve their conflictual feelings over dependency were provided through case materials.

Mendelson et al. (1957) presented nine cases of adult males with a substantial history of nonethyl (toxic) alcoholism. Observation evidenced no expression of aggressive or hostile impulses; on the contrary, highly submissive and compliant behavior was exhibited within the hospital setting. These men were described as perfect examples of "essential alcoholics" who, because of an inability to cope adequately with environmental stresses coupled with high oral needs, regress, through the ingestion of alcohol, to a level at which their needs are met and feelings of childlike omnipotence are achieved. The circle is a vicious one, for the more frustration felt toward the world for not satisfying oral needs, the more alcohol is turned to for satisfaction. Alcohol produces feelings of guilt, dependency, and need for punishment and in turn drives the alcoholic back to the bottle for the never ending search for oral need satisfaction. The findings of Mendelson et al. confirm the thesis of many professionals in the field that the rehabilitation of the alcoholic is a problem of dependency reduction. Munt (1960) pointed out that one of the major problems in carrying on casework with alcoholics stems from their strong fear of their own dependency wishes. These findings were supported in a study of Skid Row alcoholics by Perry et al. (1970).

Booth (1969) predicted that alcoholics, because of their deep-seated need for dependence, would choose dependence over self-reliance (or independence) when confronted with a choice between the two. Twenty alcoholic and 20 nonalcoholic males from a voluntary community mental health treatment center took part in a five-part experimental task. After completion of each of the five sections, they were informed as to the success of their performance. After the fifth section was completed and feedback on performance had been received by the men, they were informed that the section could be repeated, ostensibly due to experimenter error. As predicted alcoholics chose to change relatively few responses and in doing so both accepted failure and rejected the possibility of success; their nonalcoholic counterparts tried to better their performance and, thus, chose success over failure when presented a choice.

Hughes and Reuder (1968) focused on the suppressed anger component of unsatisfied dependency needs in obese women. Predicated on the assumption that latent anger would result in increased sensitivity to stimuli associated with the anger arousal object, lists of neutral and anger-related words were presented to 16 obese (200 pounds or over) and 16 nonobese women. The women were allowed certain amounts of time to alphabetize each list, after which they were asked to estimate their working time. The expectation that obese women would overestimate the time spent on lists containing anger-related words more than nonobese women was confirmed.

Most persons who are dependent are passive dependent; that is, they are merely passive recipients of the affection, help, support, etc. that others may offer. The suicidal, on the other hand, is representative of an active dependent: he actively manipulates others into a position of satisfying his needs. Based on the supposition that life style is reflected in verbal and written communications, Darbonne (1969) hypothesized that suicidals and nonsuicidals would differ in content of communications. The form of communication studied was the suicide note, actual in the cases of 40 males who had committed suicide and 31 males who had threatened suicide and simulated in the cases of 40 who were nonsuicidal. Only the findings pertaining to dependency, or to a "pampered life style," will be presented. Suicidals, significantly more often than nonsuicidals, expressed a need to have their needs fulfilled by others, a need to have emotional support from others, a tendency to have difficulty in coping with loss, and attached relatively greater importance to parents and/or authority figures. Those men who had threatened suicide, like the suicidals, expressed a need for emotional support and attributed greater importance to parental figures; they did not differ from nonsuicidals for need to have others satisfy their needs and difficulty adapting to loss. Possibly stemming from early parental handling of dependency needs, the adult who tends toward suicide may have learned that, if he is able to instill in others feelings of responsibility for harms he inflicts upon himself, others will satisfy his needs for him. Because he does not directly bring about his own need satisfaction, the suicidal is likely to be a relatively undifferentiated person and experience feelings of worthlessness.

Predicated on the assumption that aggression is more appropriately expressed by persons who have many others upon whom they can rely during times of crisis, Lester (1969) hypothesized that suicidals, whose expressions of aggression can be considered inappropriate, will have available fewer persons to whom they can turn during crisis periods and that they will have greater feelings of ambivalence toward these persons than nonsuicidals. A modification of the Situation Resources Repertory Test (RES) was given to 8 students who had reportedly threatened suicide, 6 students who had actually attempted suicide, and 30 students who reportedly had never considered suicide. The hypotheses were confirmed. Emotional disturbance was ruled out as a factor contributing to suicidal's feeling of ambivalence toward the objects of their dependency but was found to be characteristic of all students whose dispersion of dependency was small. Thus, the suicidal, during crisis situations, is faced with the problem of having to turn for help to the very persons for whom he harbors resentment.

Therapists who work with suicidal clients are often confronted with the problem of differentiating between those whose threats will culminate in suicide and those whose gestures are non-life threatening. In an attempt to provide the therapist with predictive information, Faucett et al. (1969) studied the interpersonal communications patterns among high, moderate, and low risk suicidals. On the basis of patient and family interview material, it was shown that the high risk suicidal has greater difficulty handling his need for dependence through interpersonal relationships; consequently, he is likely to remain in relative isolation from others and is thus less effectively able to utilize the emotional or instrumental support of others during crisis situations.

Chronic Illness

With an estimated 23 million chronically ill in the United States, the management of dependency in the patient suffering from chronic illness is a problem with which the field of rehabilitation is very much concerned. If dependency problems can be resolved, some chronically ill patients can be vocationally rehabilitated. Others can be rehabilitated to the level of independent living. The importance of rehabilitation for independent living has achieved increasing recognition by the health and welfare professions, not only from the standpoint of the emotional and social benefits to the patient himself, but also as a financially sound policy for the community as well. With the ever-increasing demand for medical and hospital services, staff and funding needs are becoming disconcertingly apparent. Thus, the more the number of chronically ill individuals who can become sufficiently independent to care for their own needs at home, the greater will be the ability of the institutionalized health facilities to cope with the demand and needs of the remaining chronically ill.

The dependency problems of the chronically ill are especially difficult because they are long term in nature and place those responsible for their care under prolonged stress. In many instances the chronically ill patient expresses his frustrations and resentments at his limitations by becoming excessively demanding and dependent. This syndrome is particularly noticeable in the geriatric patient.

Nichols and Bogdonoff (1962) pointed out that for the chronically ill and for his family the patient's "sick role," characterized by dependency, passivity, reduced protectiveness, and reduced demands by others, may become an "entrenched way of life." The patients may consciously or unconsciously resist the physican's effort to return the patient to a healthy role. In order to modify this resistance the authors suggest that the patient's sick role must not be initially challenged. Further, before working through with the patient his fears and anxieties, every attempt should be made to help him achieve a feeling of physical well-being. The final step is then the retraining and reeducation of the patient and his family in order that they may adjust realistically to the illness.

That patients themselves can be helped to deal with illness-caused dependency has been repeatedly demonstrated. Garner et al. (1958) reduced clinic visits of some geriatric clients by one third by introducing these patients to a medical psychiatric service. Those who benefited most were those individuals whose dependency was situational, those who were reacting realistically to temporary illness. Those who benefited least showed histories of chronic dependency.

Kutner (1966) described an experiment in the use of "therapeutic milieu" for long-term physically handicapped patients on the hospital ward. Changes instituted as part of the program included "low level" staff attendance at staff meetings, patient-staff meetings, increased family involvement, increased patient activities, and mixing of sexes on the wards. Early assessment of results pointed out such disadvantages as staff discomfort due to change in staff social structure and responsibilities as well as increased patient demands. However, benefits seemed to offset the disadvantages. Staff morale increased as did patient participation in significant activities. More important, dependency upon the hospital structure was lessened.

One area in which important inroads can be made in combatting the dependency of chronically ill patients is the nursing home. Unfortunately, many nursing homes become mere custodial institutions, thus fostering the dependency of their patients rather than fighting it. If a nursing home adopts a rehabilitation philosophy, it can do much toward the creation of a modicum of independent functioning in its patients. Margolin and Hurwitz (1962) described the existing situation in their statement:

The condition of America's nursing homes has become a major problem of the aged and aging. The demand for skilled nursing services and rehabilitation for an increased number of disabled older persons is rising and will become more intense as life expectancy increases in the next several decades.

Research by Stotsky (1969) has documented the serious dependency problems of the aged which are exacerbated in the nursing home setting.

The rehabilitation activities do not necessarily require elaborate or expensive equipment. Rather a rehabilitation attitude on the part of the staff is the ingredient which enables patients to become motivated to maintain themselves at their highest level of functioning. Staff must encourage self-care and ambulation wherever possible and design a schedule of occupational and social activities which is both challenging and gratifying to the chronic patient. In a sense the staff of the nursing home takes on the emotional aspects of a family to the patient and thus has a similar effect to that of the family in motivating the patient toward or away from dependency.

Social Disability

The rehabilitation of community-induced dependency is a crucial problem in modern society. The term "community-induced dependency" refers to that dependency produced by poverty due to lack of opportunity, and perpetuated by positive reinforcement of public welfare income maintenance.

The recent upsurge of interest in the poor by both government and voluntary organizations is not due to mere chance. It is rather the result of a philosophy which began to develop in the United States before the turn of the century when people, through their government and private organizations, began to accept some responsibility for helping those who for social, emotional, and physical reasons were unable to adjust to the stresses and demands of life. Early in the twentieth century, when such individuals were looked upon as deviants, community responsibility was limited to financial assistance or income maintenance. However, with the financial depression of the 1930's came the realization that few, if any, were immune to the buffetings of fate, illness, and psychosocial stress.

Accompanying the realization was the philosophy that, as a treatment for the dependency of poverty, the use of financial assistance alone was unsound economically and unrewarding for the individual, socially and emotionally. At this point the need to adopt a psychosocial, diagnostic and therapeutic viewpoint became evident. To fight economic disability one must first understand the reasons for the individual's dependency; then motivate him to raise his general level of functioning as a member of society; and finally provide him with the opportunity structure (training, job opportunity, and other resources) to achieve this rise to independence.

Initially the rehabilitation of the poor was attempted by caseworkers utilizing a dyadic treatment relationship with limited attempts to change the opportunity structure. However, it became increasingly recognized that, unless major attempts were made to improve the opportunities for the poor, gains in fighting the dependency of poverty would be fragmentary and minimal; hence, the development of concerted services and community action programs in which community organization techniques are used to involve the participation of the dependent poor to help themselves.

The community action programs are based on the technique of using indigenous community leaders and workers to educate, interpret, and motivate those made dependent by poverty to organize and utilize resources which will enable them to reconstruct community life in their neighborhoods and raise themselves to independent functioning. Pearl and Reissman (1965) selected a quotation from *Youth in the Ghetto* (Harlem Youth Opportunities Unlimited, Inc., 1964) which sums up the technique for involving community participation:

In a very real way the use of indigenous non-professionals in staff positions is forced by the dearth of trained professionals. At the same time, however, the use of such persons grows out of the concern for a tendency of professionals to "flee from the client" and the difficulty of communication between persons of different backgrounds and outlooks. It is HARYOU's[a] belief that the use of persons only "one step removed" from the client will improve the giving of services as well as provide useful and meaningful employment for Harlem's resident.

However, there are those who question the value of indigenous workers on the basis that after a period the indigenous worker takes on professional values, status, and aspirations and can no longer effectively communicate with the underprivileged.

Various techniques have been used to obtain community involvement and

[a]Harlem Youth Opportunities Unlimited, Inc.

cooperation of the financially handicapped. It has been reported (Gadfly of the Poverty War, 1965; Poverty Soviets, 1965; Silberman, 1964; Strength through Misery, 1965) that Saul Alinsky, one of the early proponents of community organization techniques to fight dependency, advocates the mobilization and use of power through organization of the poor as a social and political force. His (1946) dogma is:

People don't get the opportunity or freedom or equality or dignity as an act of charity. You need organization first to compel concessions and second to make the other side deliver. And people who feel trapped in no-way out poverty don't organize effectively unless someone with the requisite skill moves in, listens to their gripes, finds their real leaders, and sets them moving in showy campaigns.

Alinsky's philosophy demands that rather than accepting a handout the poor help themselves by changing the status quo through the power of their organized numbers. Based on this philosophy, he founded the Industrial Area Foundation (IAF) to fight poverty, dependency, and the slum life style. Alinsky has been invited into a number of areas and has organized numerous projects, but his "Back of the Yards" project in Chicago, started in 1939, and The Woodlawn Organization (TWO), also in Chicago, are his most well-known and successful projects. The Woodlawn Organization was a federation of 85 to 90 groups, including 13 churches, 3 businessmen's associations, and an assortment of block clubs, neighborhood associations, and social groups. The slum is directly south of the University of Chicago campus and contains anywhere from 80,000 to 150,000 inhabitants.

As concern about the life style of the poor increased so did concern about their cultural deprivation and mental health. Reissman (1964) stated that:

The greatest block to the realization of the deprived individual's creative potential appears to be his verbal inadequacies. He seems to have enormous difficulty expressing himself verbally in many situations. For example, when interviewing underprivileged individuals, one of the most characteristic comments encountered is, "You know what I mean." It is liberally appended to all kinds of answers and occurs even when the respondent is at ease with the interviewer. This difficulty takes place even at school; consequently, there has arisen a rather firm belief that the deprived child is basically inarticulate.

Reissman went on to point out that the underprivileged are not nonverbal or less verbal but verbal in a different way which relates to their own actions and culture-bound vocabulary.

There has developed among experts in the field of rehabilitation of the disadvantaged a very definite difference of opinion concerning the norms, values, and aspirations of the client. One group exemplified by Miller (1958) has postulated a specific lower class culture which is not particularly concerned with the values of the middle class. Rodman (1965) and others, on the other hand, have taken the position that the lower class values stretch to be influenced by and include those of the middle class.

During the past decade the federal government through the allocation of funds and enabling legislation has attempted to deal with dependency in the rehabilitation of the socially disabled and disadvantaged client. Various man-power training, self-help and community action programs were attempted with varying degrees of success. While some noteworthy success was achieved, for the most part, success in combating dependency in the disadvantaged client was limited. A major reason for this limited success was the blocking of real community indigenous decision-making by the power structure external to the affected community. In these cases maximum feasible participation was always a catch phrase and never a reality. Research by Craddock et al. (1970) and Spencer (1970) showed that where there was good community involvement rehabilitation of disadvantaged community members ensued.

Since the study by Hollingshead and Redlich (1958) there has been a marked rise in the interest of professionals in the mental health of the poor. In this regard an environmental viewpoint has been emerging. Duhl (1963) in describing the "Changing Face of Mental Health" proposed an ecological view. In discussing the new model, Duhl remarked:

This more comprehensive perspective is called "ecology," the study of multiple factors of environment, both internal and external, that effect normal develop-ment and behavior of the individual and his society. "Mental Health" thus becomes not the study of mental disease alone, but the study of man in society.

In summary, it can be said that the major question which arises is what techniques are best utilized to contact and reach those who are handicapped by poverty. Thus far it would appear that the aggressive offering of tangibles and the creation of an improved opportunity structure which offers possibilities for self-help hold the most promise for the rehabilitation of community-induced dependence.

Rehabilitation Counseling to Reduce Dependency

Case. Two patients, both bilateral above-knee amputees, were being treated within a rehabilitation center. One was an 82-year-old retired police chief. The other was a 23-year-old young adult. The police chief, having been called upon for a high degree of independent functioning and decision-making his earlier life, showed strong independent strivings and worked long and diligently with his corrective therapist to learn to use his prosthesis effectively. His success was remarkable and he was able to live a meaningful life.

The 23-year-old boy, on the other hand, had been greatly overprotected by an overindulgent mother who did everything for him and stifled his independent strivings at every turn. This young man absolutely refused to have corrective therapy or even try his prosthesis, let alone practice its use. No amount of persuasion or cajoling could motivate him to attempt physical restoration. Finally, as a last resort, the corrective therapist decided upon a course of action which was a calculated risk. He picked up the patient bodily in his arms and carried him down to the corrective therapy room. This act precipitated a panic state. The patient experienced extreme fear, anxiety, cried profusely and appeared to be completely emotionally shattered. The therapist then carried him back to his bed after a very brief period in the therapy room. The corrective therapist reported that for several days following the episode the patient was near psychotic in his behavior. However, as the therapist had hoped, as the initial anxiety over the incident subsided, an amazing change began to take place in the patient. He commenced, ever so slightly at first, to communicate to the corrective therapist an interest in going into therapy with him and learning to use the prosthesis. This interest increased as the patient moved into a highly dependent relationship with the therapist. The therapist was aware of the emotional transaction which was taking place and allowed this dependent relationship to develop so that he could use it as a motivational device in the patient's corrective therapy. The technique was successful. The patient did come into corrective therapy and began to adjust to his prosthesis. However, in the corrective therapy setting he was exceedingly dependent upon the therapist and would not make a move without either consulting the therapist or demanding his help. The therapist allowed this dependency to continue until the rehabilitation process itself began to take on some meaning for the patient. At this point, he began weaning the patient from his extreme dependent position. Very gradually, he compelled his patient to do little things for himself and began to make slightly jarring remarks, in which he compared the patient to other patients who did things for themselves. The patient tried desperately to cling to his dependent relationship with the therapist, but the therapist's approval of independent strivings won out and the patient began to function with a certain amount of independence. His independent functioning reached the point where he was trained and vocationally rehabilitated into a routine assembly job. Since there remained much dependency within his personality it was important to place him on a job which gave structure to his activities and close supervision. What is important, however, is that rehabilitation took place in a patient who appeared hopelessly dependent.

This case, as discussed by Margolin (unpublished paper) has been cited to illustrate that techniques utilized to rehabilitate highly dependent, handicapped individuals must vary and be based not only on psychosocial factors in the patient's immediate environment but also upon the developmental aspects of his dependency. Adequate knowledge of the early patterns of dependent behavior ongoing in the client's family relationships is of considerable importance. With the 82-year-old ex-police chief there was little need for the therapist to deal with his dependency. That dependency existed within his personality structure was undoubtedly the case. However, his characteristic style of dealing with his dependent strivings, which he had developed over a period of time, was constructive and required little in the way of motivational intervention by the corrective therapist. The 23-year-old male patient, on the other hand, had a life style of dealing with his dependent impulses which was emotionally crippling and immobilizing. Strong interventive action from an outside source was required.

There are many who would disagree with the corrective therapist's method of approach on the basis that it was overly traumatic and risked even more emotional damage to the patient than already existed. This is a valid issue. It is important, nevertheless, to point out that there was a psychodynamic rationale for the particular course of action which the therapist followed. He was utilizing a type of emotional shock therapy in which the patient's emotional homeostasis was so threatened that he was compelled to mobilize all his inner resources to make a readjustment. To accomplish this the patient had to have a certain amount of ego strength to call upon. The therapist in this case evaluated the patient's ego strength as sufficient to sustain the trauma. The patient, however, was not without support from the therapist. In bodily carrying the patient to therapy the therapist was nonverbally saying, "I am compelling you to live on a better and higher level, but you do not have to do it alone. In the same way as you depend on me as I carry you in my arms, you can depend on me through the entire process of therapy and the achievement of independence. Your freedom and independence mean enough to me to go this far." Thus, the foundation for a strong treatment relationship is set down if the patient is helped to handle the initial trauma.

Basic to the management of dependency in the handicapped client is the rehabilitation counseling process itself. Few, if any, handicapped individuals have sufficient ability to cope effectively with their own dependent strivings which encourage passivity. The counseling relationship provides the client with a psychosocial situation which allows him a testing ground to prepare him to face and cope with feelings and problems which will occur when he is confronted with stresses in the community.

There are essentially two rehabilitation procedures which have value for dealing with the pronounced dependency problems of the mental patient, particularly the chronic psychotic. The first is the provision of a strong supportive relationship with a highly skilled rehabilitation counselor who can clarify dependency problems for the patient and at the same time help him cope with the buffetings of an independent life.

Stotsky and Margolin (1957) elucidated the second technique which involves the creation of a transitional work program for the patient. This provides him with a period of time during which he has had the opportunity to work through his dependency problems in an atmosphere which slowly diminishes the security of the hospital by exposing the patient to demands for independent functioning which he will be obliged to confront when he returns to the community on a full-time basis. Specifically, this was known as the "Member-Employer Program"[b] (Peffer et al. 1957). Since space does not permit a detailed description, it is sufficient to state that it was an all-out vocational rehabilitation program which was built around the philosophy of the therapeutic value of gainful employment. This program involved as much community work and counseling with employers as it did with patients. What is of principal importance is the character of the counseling techniques developed and utilized to combat institutional dependency.

In this program the relative passivity of the therapist and non-directive counseling techniques which stem from the original work of Rogers and from psychoanalytically-oriented proponents of self-determinism were less heavily used and were, to a large extent, replaced by a strongly directive type of counseling. In this, the power of the counselor's relationship with the members was used to create confidence and to bolster the ego strength necessary to move the patient toward gainful employment away from the hospital. Failure on the part of the member-employee was accepted by the counselor without negative judgment. What was not accepted was the member's tendency to lapse back into institutional dependency and not to try again. In some instances statements which might be construed as traumatic were used by the counselor to create the reality shock necessary to motivate the member's independent strivings.

The very nature of the patient-physician relationship demands a certain amount of submission to and reliance upon the doctor by the patient in terms of the treatment plan and the means by which the rehabilitation goals can be achieved. Based on a role theory model, Ludwig and Adams (1968) postulated that clients whose previous social status and role relationships demanded similar positions of dependence and subordination would be more likely to assume a client role and successfully complete rehabilitation services than to be uncooperative or drop out of treatment prematurely. Selected for study were 406 clients at a large rehabilitation center who were evaluated as able to profit from treatment. As predicted, those clients who followed through and completed the rehabilitation plan (successful rehabilitation per se is not implied) were significantly more likely to have been female, non-white, non-middle-aged, unemployed prior to their present disabling condition, severely handicapped, referred from an agency, indebted to a voluntary or public service organization for payment of services, and favorably disposed toward the medical profession. Thus, dependency was shown to be an asset during the rehabilitation process.

The origins of neurotic dependency, its use by the patient as a defense against achieving independence, the neurotic reactions to it by some therapists who themselves have conflicts not yet resolved, and techniques of treatment were discussed by Lower (1967).

He defined what he termed "neurotic dependency" as follows:

. . . a state in which a person's sense of well-being is determined by what he receives from another, to a degree inappropriate to his stage of development. In

[b]The Member-Employee Program took place at the Veterans Administration Hospital in Brockton, Massachusetts. This was one of forty such programs conducted throughout the United States. It was discontinued for administrative reasons.

terms relevant to psychotherapy, it refers to a condition or a form of behavior in which the patient feels that he can progress only to the extent that he receives from the therapist something which he cannot possibly find within himself. He is dependent in the sense that he *leans upon* rather than *works with* the therapist, and his goal in therapy is to avoid separation rather than to gain autonomy.

In recent years clients have challenged the expertise of the helping professional, his altruistic intentions, and the effectiveness of the delivery system; in short, the client of today is less likely than his predecessor to assume a passive dependent position subservient to his doctor, social worker, or counselor (Haug and Sussman, 1969). The importance of involving the client in the decision-making process cannot be denied. However, as pointed out by Dilley (1967), the counselor is often faced with a dilemma. If the counselor in any way challenges the soundness of the client's decision, he risks alienating the client; if the counselor unconditionally accepts the client's decision when that decision does not appear to be based on reality factors, he risks perpetuating an unrealistic approach which may cost the client more than time. Dilley proposed that counselors avoid direct confrontation and, instead, help the client to think in terms of alternatives and uncertainties so as to strengthen the client's own decision-making powers.

The counselor is generally required to work with many kinds of clients within various kinds of counseling situations. The extent to which he is able to relate effectively within a wide range of client-counselor relationships often determines his success as a counselor. In a study by Gabbert et al. (1967), college males and females were seen by counselors at a university counseling center and filled out the Counseling Evaluation Inventory, Short Form, a measure of client attitude toward counselors and counseling. Client sex, length of therapy, and diagnostic category (personal-psychological vs. educational-vocational) significantly affected client attitudes toward counselors. The authors suggested that counselors examine their own behavior in light of possible effects it may have upon the client.

In a study by Farley (1968) interview and questionnaire data pertaining to client-counselor interaction were gathered on 153 rural rehabilitation clients, their families, and their male vocational rehabilitation counselors. Among the findings reported was the tendency for rehabilitation counselors to perceive their more dependent clients less favorably, especially their dependent male clients; in contrast, the more favorable attitudes toward counselors tended to have been expressed by the dependent clients. Although it was concluded that dependent clients were more difficult to rehabilitate, these same clients held more positive attitudes toward rehabilitation. It was suggested that counselors re-examine and attempt to come to terms with their own feelings about dependency in order to minimize the discrepancy in client-counselor attitude and thus better serve their clients.

Heller and Goldstein (1961) designed a study to measure the relationship between client therapy attraction and the variables of client dependency and therapist improvement expectation. Two groups of college students seeking therapy were used. The experimental group was to receive during the course of the study fifteen therapy sessions; the control group was to be placed on a waiting list. Prior to the experimental group's first therapy session and after its fifteenth session, both groups received the EPPS, the Situational Test of Dependency, and the Picture Impressions Test for measurement of self-reported dependency, behavioral dependency, and feelings toward therapists and therapy, respectively. The therapist, after every fifth session, rated his own expectation of client improvement. Results indicated that for all subjects both self-reported and behavioral dependency measures obtained prior to the experimental group's first therapy session were positively related to client pretherapy attraction. However, only behavioral dependency for the experimental group obtained after the fifteenth therapy session related significantly with client pre-therapy attraction. For both the experimental and control groups, the difference between EPPS scores obtained prior to the first and after the fifteenth session were negatively related to client pre-therapy attraction. Client self-perception, but not behavioral action, had changed after therapy. For the experimental group, pretherapy attraction was not related to therapist expectation of client improvement. Client post-therapy as well as the difference between pre- and post-therapy attraction, however, were significantly related to therapist expectation after the fifth session but not after the tenth and fifteenth sessions.

Mosey (1968) investigated the relationship between dependency (need for support from others) and integrative skill (the ability to perceive, respond to, and fulfill the needs of others) with regard to affinity for (desire for membership in the group) and acceptance by the group to which one is assigned (group's desire for the individual's presence). Dependency and integrative skill were measured by the Sixteen Personality Factor Questionnaire; affinity and acceptance, by peer ratings. Subjects were 121 occupational therapists between the ages of 22 and 60. No relationships were found between dependency, affinity, or integrative skill and acceptance by the group; a small positive relationship was noted between affinity for and dependency on the group; small negative relationships were observed between both dependency on and affinity for the group and the ability to perceive and fulfill the needs of others in the group; finally, it was found that the desire for group membership is more closely related to the need for support from others than to the group's desire for the individual.

Counseling is a diagnostically based process and the choice of counseling techniques must be determined by the situation, needs, and strengths of the particular client. However, counseling styles depend to a large extent upon the skill, training, and therapeutic school of psychology to which the particular counselor is committed. One way in which counseling styles differ is the degree of directiveness and nondirectiveness employed by the counselor in helping the handicapped client arrive at decisions.

Rottschafer (1961) studied the effect of expected counseling style on client dependency in therapy. Well motivated undergraduates were selected on the basis of the Mooney Problem Checklist. Counseling style, leading or reflective, was determined by the administration of the Strupp Scale to counselors. Results indicated that regardless of style expected students counseled with leading style produced a significantly greater proportion of dependent responses during initial counseling than students counseled by a reflective counselor. Further, regardless of style received, students expecting leading style also responded with significantly greater proportion of dependency material than students expecting reflective style. The greatest and least proportions of dependent responses were given by students expecting and receiving leading and students expecting and receiving reflective counseling styles, respectively. No differences resulted between groups induced to expect one style and receiving another and groups receiving the style expected. It was concluded that dependency in therapy is negligibly affected by induced expectations.

Since this study was based on first interviews, there is no way of knowing with certainty whether a leading style of counseling would continue to produce or increase client dependency. If a rehabilitation counselor is too directive in his style of counseling, he runs the risk of usurping the client's initiative, thus fostering or increasing dependency. On the other hand, if the counselor's directiveness is channeled toward moving the client to take steps which will call for increased independent action, the directive counseling style may turn out to be functional. Margolin (1955) in his work with the Member Employee Program found directive counseling techniques to work successfully with hospitalized mental patients. In this program vocational placement took place in 800 cases.

The importance of considering choice of counseling style in light of the personality characteristics and need structure of the client was illustrated by Gilbreath (1967, 1968) and Chestnut and Gilbreath (1969). Male undergraduate underachievers (based on a discrepancy between performance on a college entrance exam and present grade-point average) were assigned to leader-structured group counseling (directive), group-structured group counseling (non-directive), or no counseling. A measure of dependency was obtained from the Stern Activities Index. Results showed that high dependents were more likely to improve in grade-point average after having received leader-structured counseling while low dependents were more likely to improve after having received group-structured counseling. Follow-up studies indicated that the effects of counseling generally did not persist over time.

In addition to research on the effects of counseling as a function of client-counselor characteristics, job satisfaction and performance as a function of worker-supervisor attitudes has also been studied. Boyles (1968) predicted that high authoritarian workers would perform better for and express greater job satisfaction with supervisors high in "initiating structure" and that workers with a high need for independence would perform better for and express greater job satisfaction with supervisors high in "consideration." Subjects were female trunk airline reservations agents and their female supervisors. Supervisory styles and worker characteristics were determined by a questionnaire. Although the two hypotheses were not confirmed, other results were obtained. Job satisfaction was greater for high authoritarian workers regardless of supervisory style; however, greater satisfaction was expressed by high authoritarians who were also low on need for independence when they worked under supervisors who were high in initiating structure. Also, regardless of worker characteristics, job satisfaction and job performance was higher under high consideration supervisors and under supervisors who were low in initiating structure, respectively. Job satisfaction was not related to job performance which, in turn, was not related to worker-supervisor type. Although results of this study showed few relationships between worker-supervisor types and job performance and satisfaction, such could be a fruitful area of research for application in workshop assessments and placement aspects of rehabilitation counseling.

In a study by Heilbrun (1968) nineteen female and 32 male college students were rated by their therapists as to their instrumental dependence on others for problem resolution and were given the Counseling Readiness Scale (designed to differentiate continuers in therapy vs. premature terminators). In contrast to males, female continuers in therapy were therapist-rated as independent in their approach to problem solving. This finding, coupled with research which has shown that male counselors tend to be significantly more nondirective than directive with female clients (but not with males) during the early stages of therapy, led Heilbrun (1970) to test his earlier proposal that dependent persons would find a nondirective approach frustrating, in many cases to the point of terminating therapy, while relatively independent persons, able to provide their own structure to the therapy situation, would find the nondirective therapist an asset. It was hypothesized that females who continue in therapy do so because of the nondirectiveness of the therapist. The Counseling Readiness Scale and the Interviewer Response Preference Task (scored to reflect both preference for directiveness vs. nondirectiveness and the strength of the preference) were administered to 43 college females. The results confirmed expectations.

Jacobson (1969) tested the relative effectiveness of "instructions" and "models" upon the interview material elicited by high and low dependent college students. Subjects were divided into four groups of 30 on the basis of sex and EPPS dependency and were interviewed twice. Prior to the first interview each subject was instructed to talk about what he was like as a person (self discussion), talk about his problems (problem discussion), or to listen to one of three 10-minute tapes, each serving as a model of self discussion, problem discussion, or problem discussion in which the interviewee projected the feeling of having difficulty relating his problems. Dependency groups did not differ during the first interview for problem or self discussion but during the second interview (one week later) high dependent subjects were able to maintain their rate of self discussion whereas the low dependents were not. For problem discussion, the direct requests or instructions to divulge problems proved more effective during the initial interview for all subjects but during the second interview there was no difference between instructions for or models of problem discussion for the high dependency group. Self discussion was best for all subjects when they had been exposed to tapes containing examples of self discussion. Finally, high dependents who were instructed to divulge problems had greater difficulty in problem expression than did low dependents.

Siddigi (1968) studied changes in peer acceptance as a function of changes in dependency and hostility among fifth and sixth graders. Twenty-nine children who were rated by their classmates as low in sociometric status and who volunteered to participate in six client-centered counseling sessions over a three-week period served as subjects. The first and last taped interviews were scored for client dependency, hostility, or "other" responses and for therapist approach, avoidance, or "other" response to the client statement. Client-centered counselors, as might be expected, approached dependency and hostility indiscriminately and, thus, reinforced whatever response dominated within the client's response hierarchy. Peer acceptance correlated positively with increased dependency and decreased hostility behavior. Client-centered therapy benefited, then, those children whose pre-therapy behavior was more socially acceptable.

McBride et al. (1970) described the adolescent's struggle to achieve independence from his parents. Dependence was defined as "the failure to differentiate two or more egos, or the undifferentiation of an ego from the group," and independence as "having distinct ego boundaries, so that the person can distinguish his own choice from others." During childhood the youngster is principally an extension of his parents' attitudes and feelings, but with the coming of adolescence the young person is often confronted with conflicting value systems—that of his parents and that of his peers. If the resolution of the independence-dependence conflict is unsuccessful and professional help is required, the authors suggested a nondirective approach with supportive interpretations whereby the adolescent is encouraged to define himself as an individual entity, both a part of and apart from his parents and significant others.

Caracena (1965) reported that the more experienced therapists (4 or more years of experience) were more likely to approach client dependency in the initial stages of therapy than were the less experienced counselors (one year experience or less). Bohn (1967) found that training affected the directiveness of counselor response to hostile clients more than to dependent clients. Graduate students in counseling psychology responded to statements made at various points on tapes of "typical," "hostile," and "dependent" clients (male college students) both prior to and after a one-semester course on counseling techniques. During both administrations counselors responded most directively to the dependent client and least directively to the typical client. However, counselor directiveness decreased significantly during the post-course administration but not toward the dependent client. In addition to demonstrating the effects of a particular training program, the study showed that the same counselor may respond differently to different clients, at least in terms of directiveness.

Based on a content analysis of 42 fifth interviews for counselor approach-avoidance behavior to client (college students) dependence and hostility, Hartzell (1967) presented preliminary evidence demonstrating that counselor experience-training levels and nurturance-aggression need strengths (EPPS) affected counselor handling of client dependence and hostility. Of particular interest was the finding that appropriate handling of dependency was, to a greater extent than hostility, learned. Counselor training programs might, thus, consider making greater efforts to teach students how to appropriately handle client hostility as well as their own need for aggression.

The procedure proposed by Bandura et al. (1960) for scoring verbal interactions between patient and therapist has since been used by many researchers interested in the effect of therapist response upon client behavior. Briefly, the basic scoring unit was a client-counselor interaction sequence consisting of the client statement, the counselor response to it, and the patient response which immediately followed. If the researcher were interested in client dependency, each client statement would be rated as dependent or nondependent. The object of the client's dependency could also be noted. If the client statement were labeled dependent, the therapist response to it would be classified as one of the following: (1) an approach response, designed to elicit from the client further expressions of dependency (approval, exploration, instigation, reflection, labeling); (2) an avoidance response, designed to inhibit or discourage further expressions of dependency (disapproval, topical transition, silence, ignoring, mislabeling); or (3) a response irrelevant to (1) and (2). A similar scoring system, designed specifically for analyzing client dependency, can be found in Snyder (1963).

Winder et al. (1962) studied the effects of therapist approach-avoidance of client dependency on subsequent client dependency-related material. Clients were 16 mothers and 7 fathers who received counseling from psychology graduate students at a child guidance center. Data from the first two therapy sessions, content coded according to Bandura et al. (1960), showed that therapist approach to client dependency maintained or increased its subsequent occurrence while avoidance of client dependency by the therapist resulted in a decrease. Further, parents who were positively reinforced for dependency-related material tended to have received at least twenty counseling sessions whereas those who were negatively reinforced for dependency expressions tended to have dropped out of therapy after ten or fewer sessions.

Caracena (1965) argued that the results obtained by Winder et al. showed that therapist approach to client dependency served only to elicit further dependency expressions, not reinforce or strengthen client dependency. He attempted to differentiate between elicitation of an already existing dependency response and reinforcement or strengthening of that response. Seventy-two tapes of initial therapy sessions involving male and female undergraduates and therapists of three experience levels were content analyzed according to Bandura et al. (1960). The results supported Winder et al. for further elicitation of client dependency-related material following therapist approach but did not support Winder et al. for the relationship between therapist approach to client dependency expressions and "remainers" in therapy. More importantly, the data did not support a reinforcement position: neither an increased probability of the client's continuing with nor of his initiating dependency topics as a function of therapist approach to client dependency was found.

Similarly, data obtained by Schuldt (1966) did not support a reinforcement position. His clients were 16 college students who were seen by 13 therapists of two experience levels. Five interviews representing the first, last, and intermediate stage of therapy (selected proportionately on the basis of length of therapy) were content coded according to a modified Bandura et al. (1960) scoring procedure. The results were as follows: 1) therapists approached (i.e., approved, supported) dependency related to the client's feelings about the therapist more than dependency of the client toward others; 2) therapists tended to approach client dependency at a constant rate throughout all phases of therapy; 3) clients tended to follow through with references to dependency when approved by the therapist and to avoid the subject when the therapist did (i.e., disapproved, ignored); 4) clients introduced dependency themes more often during the initial stages of therapy than during later phases; 5) there was little difference between experienced therapists and less experienced therapists in regard to approaching dependency in initial phases of psychotherapy. At a later time Schuldt (1968) reanalyzed these data in terms of high and low therapist approach rate to client dependency. Although no differences in probability of continuing dependency topics as a function of therapist rate of approach to client dependency were found, client-initiated dependency statements occurred significantly more frequently when therapist rate of approach was high. These studies, then, show that the therapist does elicit an already existing dependency response from the client but whether or not he serves to strengthen his client's dependency remains questionable.

Operant conditioning techniques have been successfully used to reduce dependence in the small group situation. Orlando (1969) administered to 24 40- to 50-year-old institutionalized veterans the Navran Dependence Scale (MMPI) and the Supervisors Performance Evaluation prior to and following 16 one-hour small group counseling sessions. Half the groups received positive reinforcement for verbalizations denoting independence. Decreases in posttest dependence positively correlated with increases in statements of independence during counseling and were found to occur more prevalently among the younger, shorter term institutionalized men. Whether or not these changes persisted over time was not ascertained. The authors suggest that there is a definite need for more extensive and rigorous research in the area of operant conditioning as it affects dependency. Such knowledge would be helpful to practitioners in all phases of the rehabilitation process.

In order to more fully understand the significance of the content aspects of client-counselor interactions during therapy, it is necessary to take into consideration the personality of both client and counselor and to interpret content in light of what each brings with him to the interview. Heller et al. (1963) investigated the effects of client personality upon counselor behavior. Thirty-four interviewers, all graduate students in psychology, were seen for one half hour by each of four student actors trained to play one of the following client roles: dependent-hostile, dependent-friendly, dominant-hostile, dominant-friendly. Results confirmed the hypotheses that counselor affect (hostility vs. friendliness) will mirror client affect and that client control (dependency vs. dominance) will result in opposite control behavior on the part of the counselor. The possibility should not be overlooked that more experienced counselors may have better learned how to handle their own impulses and, thus, may be less affected by client behavior.

Houts et al. (1969) made a preliminary investigation of the perceptual and behavioral interdependence between patient and therapist. At a rotating patient outpatient clinic, where patients do not see the same therapist each week, seven patients saw each of four therapists twice. After each session, therapists rated on 4-point scales how they thought the patient should behave and how they thought they should behave to accomplish the goals of therapy. All sessions were taped and actual patient and therapist behaviors were rated according to the same 4-point scales by two judges. One of the major findings was a discrepancy between what therapists thought should occur and what actually did occur in terms of patient behavior. Patients, not therapists, were the key determinants of both patient and therapist behavior and even influenced the way the therapists thought they themselves should behave. The authors pointed out that the generalization potential of their study is very limited due to the small sample size and unusual type of therapy employed.

Dependency changes during psychotherapy were also studied by Alexander and Abeles (1968, 1969). Ten male and 10 female college student clients obtained 10 to 20 one-hour interviews over a 6- to 30-week period from male therapists at a university counseling center. In order to assess sex differences, clients were administered the MMPI prior to therapy. Tapes of the first, middle and next-to-last interviews were scored for client dependency (Bandura, et al., 1960) and for object of client dependency (Lennard and Bernstein, 1960). After the termination of therapy, the counselors rated their clients' success in therapy. It was assumed that the frequency of client dependency statements would decrease as a function of conflict resolution during therapy. Results showed that client dependency on the therapist increased while dependency upon his family decreased from the beginning to the midpoint of therapy. By the end of therapy, client dependency on his peer group also decreased but dependence on the therapist remained at the same level. Thus, the client was described as transferring his dependence on his parents to the therapist but was unable, within the time allowed, to adequately work through the transference experience to the point of successfully handling his own dependency needs. Alexander and Abeles portrayed the therapy process as representing "a compact developmental experience."

Males and females did not differ in terms of frequency of dependency statements. MMPI data showed that males generally scored above the norm and toward the feminine end of the masculinity-femininity distribution, suggesting the possibility of a passive personality component in males who seek counseling. The tendency of many therapists to perceive females as more dependent than males may result in inappropriate treatment approaches if, in fact, no sex differences exist. In terms of therapist rating of client success, clients who were rated as successful tended to make fewer dependency statements and remained in therapy longer than clients rated as unsuccessful. The ability of the therapist to handle the client's intense dependency demands appears to be crucial in preventing early termination and increasing the probability of a successful therapy. Role expectations both on the part of the therapist and on the part of the client must also be considered as factors important in the therapist-client relationship.

In assessing the work of several other writers, Bordin (1965) found that patients who were overtly-dependent were helped by high commitment of the therapist in the early stages of psychotherapy while counter-dependent patients were not. The author defined overtly-dependent patients as those who showed insatiability in their need for help from the therapist, "a hostile and demanding manner," a perception of other people as cold and ungiving, and a desire to be "led by the therapist." Counter-dependent patients were described as tending to resist the therapist's help—even to the point of competing with him—and tended to perceive others as "over-solicitous and interfering."

Ahmad (1961) studied therapist-client interaction patterns with respect to client dependency. Data was based upon interviews of 23 patients seen twice each by 18 psychotherapists. Patient dependency behavior and therapist reaction to such behavior was recorded. It was found that therapists who approved of expressions of dependency retained their clients in therapy longer than those who disapproved. Moreover, clients whose dependency responses were approved of tended to express their dependency needs and conflicts over these needs more so than did clients whose dependency was rejected by the therapist. Such rejection was found to inhibit expression of feelings about dependency and result in earlier termination of treatment. Personality factors other than dependency did not appear to affect client reaction to therapist response to dependency. It was concluded that the need to work out conflict over dependency is crucial.

Winnicott (1963) related dependency in the transference situation to the dependency of the infant and child during his various developmental stages. The therapist, in order to help the patient, has to permit some dependence as well as having to interpret the transference. Since both psychosis and character disorder are due to the failure on the part of the individual's environment to provide for his psychological needs, it is important that the therapist allow the client to regress to that unsatisfied stage. Once this process is completed the client will have developed the independence necessary for his rejection of the therapist's support.

One problem often confronting the counselor or therapist is terminating the patient relationship. In order to reduce client dependency on the therapist and on the hospital and to facilitate patient return to community living, Schapira (1970) reduced then discontinued individual psychotherapy while simultaneously involving his six patients in group therapy, both with and without the patient's family members. The four patients who continued in this project and whose dependence on the hospital was an obvious block to rehabilitation initially resisted the group sessions through fear of exposing themselves to each other and to family and to ensure continued hospitalization. However, sociometric questionnaires filled out by the patients before and after the three-month period of group therapy as well as patient self ratings and ratings by their family members demonstrated improvements in social adjustment and attitude toward group therapy.

Stotsky (1963) posed these questions regarding the nature of therapy:

Will we have the sublime faith of Rogers and Allen in the individual's will to grow, or will we nudge him along? Will we increase his dependency by nudging him? Have counselors and psychotherapists discouraged initiative and increased passivity in their clients? It would be worthwhile to study the effects of counseling by contrast with no counseling on the later performance of matched groups of patients.

This chapter has attempted to analyze the relationship between dependency as a personality attribute and the process of rehabilitation. The meaning of dependency in rehabilitating patients with various types of disability was dealt with. Functional and dysfunctional aspects of dependency in rehabilitation were pointed up and discussed.

Implications for Rehabilitation

Four basic principles for combating excessive dependency may be followed in counseling the client during the rehabilitation process:

1. The counselor must be able to accept the client's dependency and communicate this to the client. He should universalize dependency for the client as a natural part of the handicap which is based in reality and which must be realistically confronted. In this way the client's guilt feelings concerning his need to depend upon others are reduced somewhat, and he can begin to resolve his conflicts over his increased need for help.

2. The counselor should focus on communicating to the client his confidence that the client can be successful in reducing his dependence on others through the process of rehabilitation. Frequently, this confidence on the part of the counselor is picked up and shared by the client. Such confidence should be realistically based upon the client's rehabilitation potential. The counselor must be prepared to encounter some resistance on the part of the disabled individual to relinquish his dependent role, since, in this role, he achieves a measure of security. His basic safety and psychological needs as stated by Maslow (1954) should be met. Movement toward independence through rehabilitation evokes anxiety because of the unpredictability of the future. The client can be helped to feel that dependence upon the counseling relationship to achieve independent functioning through rehabilitation is permissible.

3. When the counseling relationship is sufficiently well developed to support the client's ego through periods of heightened anxiety, the counselor can take the opportunity to clarify elements of dependent feelings due to family relationships, past behavior patterns, etc.

4. The counselor can help the client select those resources whose structure and staffing are best suited to help a particular client deal with his dependency needs. For example, if a sheltered workshop is indicated as a transitional dependency-reducing experience for a client, the one selected should present the client with a work milieu which best serves to decrease dependency.

In addition to helping the client cope directly with his dependency problems in certain situations, it is almost imperative that counseling be undertaken with members of the client's family as well. If members of the handicapped person's family are fostering or encouraging dependency in the client, the counselor's efforts may well be sabotaged. In some instances such dependency-producing overprotection may arise from the family members' anxiety over possible aggravation of the client's physical or mental condition. This situation is frequently corrected by interpreting the true nature of the patient's illness or handicap and reassuring the family in regard to the client's capacity and rehabilitation potential. On the other hand, some overprotection of the client by family members stems from deeper emotional problems for which the counselor must attempt to bring therapeutic help.

It is important to recognize that dependency in the client undergoing rehabilitation is a pervasive force. To some degree it has its origin in the psychodynamic development of the client's personality. Other dependency forces are precipitated by the illness or handicap itself. Individuals in the client's immediate environment influence and direct the client's dependent expressions. Community reactions also are determinants of the course which the handicapped individual's dependent actions will follow. The rehabilitation counselor is called upon to assess all these factors in helping the client work out and follow through on a rehabilitation plan.

The success of the client's rehabilitation depends upon the skill employed by the counselor in resolving his client's dependency conflict. The problems involved are complex, particularly so because rehabilitation is a compound process characterized by overlapping and interacting phases. In each phase the client's dependency differs in degree and manner of expression. For example, during diagnosis the client may deny his dependency because of social desirability factors. During physical or psychiatric restoration, dependency may take on a highly regressive character, particularly if the patient's expectations are unrealistic. In training, the relationship of instructor to client engenders a different manifestation of dependency. If training takes place in a sheltered workshop type of setting, the setting itself can stimulate dependence. During the placement process client fears and anxieties can precipitate dependent strivings so strong as to immobilize him partially or even completely.

Dependency occurring within the rehabilitation process is a constantly changing phenomena and must be evaluated at frequent intervals by the counselor. In some situations it is necessary to foster dependency initially in order to achieve a helping relationship. In other situations the dependent relationship must be diluted by diffusing dependency among a number of authority figures rather than one. In any event, the weaning of the dependent client is a gradual and calculated process.

The dependency literature has suggested that counselor attitudes are important. The authors have noted, for example, that counselors who work with a preponderance of one disability begin to feel that this disability is the most difficult to rehabilitate and the most difficult for the client to endure. Counselors who think this way help to create a dependency-prone environment which will hinder the positive motivation of their clients.

Finally, the practitioner must remain aware that there are no simple answers to client dependency. The dependence of each client will vary in accordance with his own psychodynamic structure, the determinants of his culture, and the stresses and pressures of the milieu in which he finds himself at a given time. Thus, the approach to the resolution of a client's dependency problems must be highly diagnostic in character. However, a sound background in dependency theory and research can be valuable to the practitioner in understanding the mechanics of his client's dependency so that diagnosis can be accurate and treatment effective.

In summary, the purpose of this work has been to survey existing research on dependency and to organize this material in a manner useful to professionals in the field of rehabilitation. It becomes evident from the literature that dependency is difficult to define, conceptualize, and measure. The need for further research and innovation in practice is clear. Primarily four basic research techniques have been utilized: psychometric tests, laboratory behavioral measures, ratings, and descriptions of life performance. Combinations of research techniques with large numbers of subjects could yield valid and reliable results.

For the practitioner and researcher in the field of rehabilitation much can be learned about dependency by studying it in the setting, situation, or context in which it occurs. A classification of expressions of dependency was offered based upon this point of view.

Clinical studies have indicated that while dependence may be created by the reality situation imposed by illness and handicap, the course which it follows is influenced by a number of variables. These factors include attitudes of family and friends, community acceptance, and the relationship of professionals and others who comprise the therapeutic milieu of the patient.

Bibliography

Bibliography

Adevai, Greta; Silverman, A.J.; and McGough, W.E. "MMPI Findings in Field Dependent and Field Independent Subjects." *Perceptual & Motor Skills,* 1968, 26 (1), 3-8.

Adler, P.T. "The Relationship of Two Types of Dependency to the Effectiveness of Approval as a Reinforcer Among a Group of Emotionally Disturbed Children." *Dissertation Abstracts,* 1962, 23, 697.

Ahmad, F.Z. "Aspects of Psychotherapy Related to Psychotherapists' Responses to Dependency." *Dissertation Abstracts,* 1961, 21, 3519.

Ainsworth, M.D. "Object Relations, Dependency, and Attachment: A Theoretical Review of the Infant-Mother Relationship." *Child Development,* 1969, 40 (4), 969-1025.

Ainsworth, M.D. "The Development of Infant-Mother Attachment." Edited by B.M. Caldwell, and H.N. Ricciuti. In *Review of Child Development Research,* Vol. 3. University of Chicago Press, 1970.

Alexander, J.F. "Perspectives of Psychotherapy Process: Dependency, Interpersonal Relationships, and Sex Differences." *Dissertation Abstracts,* 1968, 28 (12-B), 5197.

Alexander, James F. and Abeles, N. "Dependency Changes in Psychotherapy as Related to Interpersonal Relationships." *Journal of Consulting and Clinical Psychology,* 1968, 32 (6), 685-689.

Alexander J.F. and Abeles, N. "Psychotherapy Process: Sex Differences and Dependency." *Journal of Counseling Psychology,* 1969, 16 (3), 191-196.

Alinski, S.D. *Reveille for Radicals.* University of Chicago Press, 1946.

Asch, S.E. "Studies in the Principles of Judgment and Attitudes." *Journal of Social Psychology,* 1940, 12, 433-465.

Astrup, Anna M. "Repeated Short-Term Sensory Reduction in Mining." *Perceptual & Motor Skills,* 1968, 27 (3, Pt. 1), 863-869.

Bailey, W.; Hustmyer, F.; and Kristofferson, A. "Alcoholism, Brain Damage and Perceptual Dependence." *Quarterly Journal of Studies on Alcohol,* 1961, 22, 387-393.

Bandura, A.; Lipsher, D.H.; and Miller, P.E. "Psychotherapists Approach Avoidance Reactions to Patients' Expressions of Hostility." *Journal of Consulting Psychology,* 1960, 24, 1-8.

Bandura, A. and Walters, R. *Adolescent Aggression.* New York: Ronald Press, 1959.

Barclay, A. and Cusumano, D.R. "Father-Absence, Cross-Sex Identity, and Field Dependent Behavior in Male Adolescents." *Child Development,* 1967, 38 (1), 243-50.

Barr, Harriet L. "Relations Between Mode of Perception and Tendency to Conform. *Dissertation Abstracts,* 1968, 28 (11-B), 4741.

Barron, F. "Some Personality Correlates of Independence of Judgment." *Journal of Personality*, 1953, 21, 287-297.

Barrett, G.V. and Thornton, C.L. "Cognitive Style Differences Between Engineers and College Students." *Perceptual & Motor Skills*, 1967, 25 (3), 789-793.

Barry, H. Jr.; Barry, H. III; and Lindemann, E. "Dependency in Adult Patients Following Early Maternal Bereavement." *Journal of Nervous & Mental Disorders*, 1965, 140, 196-206.

Bateson, P.P.G. "The Characteristics and Context of Imprinting." *Biological Review*, 1966, 41, 177-220.

Beller, E.K. "Dependent and Autonomous Achievement Striving Related to Orality and Anality in Early Childhood." *Child Development*, 1957, 28, 287-315.

Beller, E.K. and Turner, J.L. "Personality Correlates of Children's Perception of Human Size." *Child Development*, 1964, 35, 441-449.

Benedict, Ruth. "Continuities and Discontinuities in Cultural Conditioning." In *Personality in Nature, Society and Culture* (2nd ed.), edited by C. Kluckohn, H.A. Murray, and D.M. Schneider. New York: Alfred A. Knopf, 1959. Pp. 530-531.

Berg, I., Nichols, K. and Pritchard, C. "School phobia: Its Classification and Relationship to Dependency." *Journal of Child Psychology and Psychiatry and Allied Disciplines*, 1969, 10 (2), 123-141.

Bergen, B.J. and Thomas, C.S. "An Attempt to Examine the Perception of Self and Hospital among Chronically Ill Mental Patients." *International Journal of Social Psychiatry*, 1969, 15 (4), 307-313.

Bernardin, A.C. and Jessor, B.A. "A Construct Validation of EPPS with Respect to Dependency." *Journal of Consulting Psychology*, 1957, 21, 63-67.

Bloom, M., Blenkner, M. & Markus, E. "Exploring Predictors of Differential Impact of Relocation on the Infirm Aged." *Proceedings of the 77th Annual Convention of the American Psychological Association*, 1969, 4 (Pt. 2), 731-732.

Bohn, M.J., Jr. "Therapist Responses to Hostility and Dependency as a Function of Training." *Journal of Consulting Psychology*, 1967, 31 (2), 195-198.

Booth, Kerry G. "The Need of Male Alcoholics to Maintain a Dependency Status and Avoid Self-Reliance." *Dissertation Abstracts International*, 1969, 30 (4-B), 1893.

Bordin, E.S. "The Ambivalent Quest for Independence." *Journal of Consulting Psychology*, 1965, 12, 339-345.

Boyles, B.R. "The Interaction Between Certain Personality Variables and Perceived Supervisory Styles and Their Relation to Performance and Satisfaction." *Dissertation Abstracts*, 1968, 28 (11-B), 4788-4789.

Braginsky, B.M. "The Relationship between Direct and Indirect Expressions of Dependency and Overt Dependent Behavior." *Dissertation Abstracts*, 1965, 26, 4849.

Brilhart, Barbara L. "Speaker-message Perception and Attitude Change of Listeners as a Function of Field-Independence." *Dissertation Abstracts*, 1966, 27 (5-A), 1462.

Brilhart, B.L. "Relationships of Speaker-message Perception to Perceptual Field Independence." *Journal of Communication*, 1970, 20 (2), 153-166.

Brudbard, L. "Dependence, Denial of Dependence and Group Conformity." *Dissertation Abstracts*, 1964, 25, 3095.

Bruell, J.H. and Peszczynski, M.D. "Perception of Verticality in Hemiplegic Patients in Relation to Rehabilitation." *Clinical Orthopaedics* 1958, 12, 124-130.

Buell, B. *Community Planning for Human Services*. New York: Columbia University Press, 1952. Pp. 412-413.

Burdick, J. Alan. "A Field-independent Alcoholic Population." *Journal of Psychology*, 1969, 73 (2), 163-166.

Buskirk, Martha; Cunningham Julie; and Kent, Carolyn A. "Disturbed Children: Therapeutic Approaches to Separation and Individuation. *American Journal of Occupational Therapy*, 1968, 22 (4), 289-293.

Cairns, R.B. "The Influence of Dependency-anxiety of the Effectiveness of Social Reinforcers." *Dissertation Abstracts*, 1960, 20, 4436.

Cairns, R.B. and Lewis, M. "Dependency and Reinforcement Value of a Verbal Stimulus." *Journal of Consulting Psychology*, 1962, 26, 1-8.

Caracena, Philip F. "Elicitation of Dependency Expressions in the Initial Stage of Psychotherapy." *Journal of Counseling Psychology*, 1965, 12 (3), 268-274.

Carrigan, W. "Stress and Psychological Differentiation." *Dissertation Abstracts*, 1967, 28 (3-B), 1185-1186.

Cartwright, D. and Zander, A. *Group Dynamics: Research and Theory*. New York: Harper and Row, 1962.

Chestnut, W. & Gilbreath, S. "Differential Group Counseling with Male College Underachievers: A Three Year Follow-Up." *Journal of Counseling Psychology*, 1969, 16 (4), 365-367.

Clapp, W.F. "Dependence and Competence in Children: Parental Treatment of Four-Year-Old Boys." *Dissertation Abstracts*, 1967, 28 (4-B), 1703.

Clark, S.L. "Authoritarian Attitudes and Field Dependence." *Psychological Reports*, 1968, 22 (1), 309-310.

Coburn, H.H. Dependency—Cause and Effect." *Journal of Rehabilitation*, 1963, 29 (5), 19.

Cohn, M.L. "Field Dependence-Independence and Reading Comprehension." *Dissertation Abstracts*, 1968, 29 (2-A), 476-477.

Collins, L.G. "Pain Sensitivity and Ratings of Childhood Experience." *Perceptual & Motor Skills*, 1965, 21, 349-350.

Comrey, A.L. and Schlesinger, B. "Verification and Extension of a System of Personality Dimensions." *Journal of Applied Psychology*, 1962, 46, 257-262.

Corah, Norman L. "Differentiation in Children and Their Parents." *Journal of Personality,* 1965, 33 (2), 300-308.

Cotler, S.; Quilty, R.E.; and Palmer, R.J. "Measurement of Appropriate and Unnecessary Help-seeking Dependent Behavior." *Journal of Consulting and Clinical Psychology*, 1970, 35 (3), 324-327.

Craddock, G.W.; Davis, C.E.; and Moore, J.L. *Social Disadvantagement and Dependency: A Community Approach.* Lexington, Massachusetts: Heath Lexington, 1970.

Cramond, W.A. "Renal Homotransplantation: Some Observations on Recipients and Donors." *British Journal of Psychiatry*, 1967, 113 (504), 1223-1230.

Cross, Herbert. "The Relation of Parental Training to Conceptual Structure in Preadolescents." *Journal of Genetic Psychology*, 1970, 116 (2), 197-202.

Cubelli, G.E. *Handicapped Fathers in ADC Families: A Study of 32 Handicapped Fathers in ADC Programs of Boston Department of Public Welfare.* Harvard School of Public Health, August 6, 1962.

Cubelli, G.E. *The Rehabilitation Program of the Division of Services Bureau of Social Welfare.* State of Maine Department of Health. Harvard School of Public Health, August 30, 1962.

Cummings, V.; Kutner, B.; and Rommey, L. "Mobilization for Maturity." *Journal of Rehabilitation*, 1969, 35 (1), 37-38.

Darbonne, A.R. "Study of Psychological Content in the Communications of Suicidal Individuals." *Journal of Consulting and Clinical Psychology*, 1969, 33 (5), 590-596.

Deever, S.G. "Ratings of Task-Oriented Expectancy for Success as a Function of Internal Control and Field Independence." *Dissertation Abstracts*, 1968, 29 (1-B), 365.

Devos, G.A. "A Quantitative Approach to Affective Symbolism in Rorschach Responses." *Journal of Projective Techniques*, 1952, 16, 133-150.

DiBartolo, R. and Vinacke, W.E. "Relationship Between Adult Nurturance and Dependency and Performance of the Preschool Child." *Developmental Psychology*, 1969, 1 (3), 247-251.

Dilley, J.S. "Decision-making: A Dilemma and a Purpose for Counseling." *Personnel and Guidance Journal*, 1967, 45 (6), 547-551.

DiStefano, J.J. "Interpersonal Perceptions of Field Independent and Field Dependent Teachers and Students." *Dissertation Abstracts International*, 1970, 31 (1-A), 463-464.

Doherty, Anne. "The Relationship of Dependency and Perception of Parents to the Development of Feminine Sex Role and Conscience." *Dissertation Abstracts*, 1969, 30 (5-B), 2415-2416.

Dubois, T.E. and Cohen, W. "Relationship between Measures of Psychological Differentiation and Intellectual Ability." *Perceptual & Motor Skills*, 1970, 31 (2), 411-416.

DuHamel, T.R. and Biller, H.B. "Parental Imitation and Nonimitation in Young Children." *Developmental Psychology*, 1969, 1 (6), 772.

Duhl, L.J. *The Urban Condition*. New York: Basic Books, 1963.

Eininger, M.A. and Hill, J.P. "Instrumental and Affectional Dependency and Nurturance in Preschool Children." *Journal of Genetic Psychology*, 1969, 115, 277-284.

Eisenberg L. "A Developmental Approach to Adolescence." *Children*, 1965, 12, 131-135.

Endsley, R. and Hartup, W. "Dependence and Performance by Pre-School Children on a Socially Reinforced Task" (abstract). *American Psychologist*, 1960, 15, 399.

Erikson, E.H. "Growth and Crisis of the 'Healthy Personality'." In *Personality in Nature, Society and Culture* (2nd ed.), edited by C. Kluckohn; H.A. Murray; and D.M. Schneider. New York: Alfred A. Knopf, 1959. 25-63.

Farley, O.W. "Variables Relating to Client-counselor Interaction in Vocational Rehabilitation." *Dissertation Abstracts*, 1968, 29 (5-A), 1448-1449.

Farr, Roberta S. "Personality Variables and Problem-solving Performance." *Dissertation Abstracts*, 1969, 29 (8-A), 2561-2562.

Faucett, J., Leff, M., and Bunney, W.E. Jr. "Suicide." *Archives of General Psychiatry*, 1969, 21 (2), 129-137.

Ferman, L. A. "Employability and Rehabilitation." In *Research Utilization Conference on Rehabilitation in Poverty Settings*, edited by R. J. Margolin and G.J. Goldin. Northeastern Studies in Vocational Rehabilitation, May, 1969, pp. 73-80.

Fishbein, G.M. "Perceptual Modes and Asthmatic Symptoms: An Application of Witkin's Hypothesis." *Journal of Consulting Psychology*, 1963, 27, 54-58.

Fitzgerald, B.J. "Some Relationships among Projective Test, Interview, and Sociometric Measures of Dependent Behavior." *Journal of Abnormal & Social Psychology*, 1958, 56, 199-203.

Flanders, N.A.; Anderson, J.P.; and Amidon, E.J. "Measuring Dependence Proneness in the Classroom." *Educational & Psychological Measurement*, 1961, 21, 575-587.

Fleener, D.E. "Attachment Formation in Human Infants." *Dissertation Abstracts*, 1968, 28 (11-B), 4774.

Ford, C.V.; Glober, G.A.; and Castelnuovo-Tedesco, P. "A Psychiatric Study of Patients with Regional Enteritis." *Journal of the American Medical Association*, 1969, 208 (2), 311-315.

Fordyce, W.E. "Application of a Scale of Dependency to Concepts of Self, Ideal-Self, Mother, and Father." *Dissertation Abstracts*, 1953, 13, 591.

Frank, Kenneth. "Mood Differentiation and Psychological Differentiation." *Dissertation Abstracts*, 1968, 28 (12-B), 5203-5204.

Freeman, H.E. and Simmons, O.G. *Mental Patient Comes Home*. New York: John Wiley, 1965.

French, Jacqueline. "Dependency Behavior and Feelings of Rejection in Aggressive and Non-aggressive Boys." *Dissertation Abstracts*, 1964, 25, 3108.

Furman, S.S. (ed.) *Reaching the Unreached*. New York: New York City Youth Board, 1962.

Gabbert, K.H.; Ivey, A.E.; and Miller, C.D. "Counselor Assignment and Client Attitude." *Journal of Counseling Psychology*, 1967, 14 (2), 131-136. "Gadfly of the Poverty War." *Newsweek*, 1965, 66, 30.

Garner, H.H., Simon, A.J.; and Handelson, M.S. "Management of Chronic Dependency in Out-Patient Clinics by a Comprehensive Medical Psychiatry Service." *Journal of the American Geriatric Society*, 1958, 6, 623-631.

Gary, Melvin L. "Field Dependence and Susceptibility to Social Influence." *Dissertation Abstracts*, 1968, 28 (12-B), 5190-5191.

Gavalas, R.C. and Briggs, P.F. "Concurrent Schedules of Reinforcement: A New Concept in Dependency." *Merrill-Palmer Quarterly*, 1966, 12, 97-121.

Gerai, J.E. "Support of Judgmental Independence or Conformity in Situations of Exposure to Strong Group Pressure." *Dissertation Abstracts*, 1959, 20, 3413.

Gilbreath, S.H. "Group Counseling, Dependence, and College Male Underachievers." *Journal of Counseling Psychology*, 1967, 14 (5), 449-453.

Gilbreath, S.H. "Appropriate and Inappropriate Group Counseling with Academic Underachievers." *Journal of Counseling Psychology*, 1968, 15 (6), 506-11.

Goffman, E. "The Characteristics of Total Institutions." In *Complex Organizations*, edited by A. Etzioni. New York: Holt, Rhinehart, and Winston, 1964, 312-340.

Goldin, G.J.; Margolin, R.J.; and Stotsky, B.A. "The Function of Group Work Techniques in the Rehabilitation of the Poverty-bound Client." Publication pending.

Goldin, G.J. "Physical vs. Mental Handicap: Contrasting Attitudes." New England Rehabilitation Research Institute, Northeastern University, Boston, Mass. Unpublished paper.

Goldin, G.J. "The Role of the Physical Therapist in Meeting the Psychological Needs of Handicapped Children." Brandeis University, Waltham, Mass. Unpublished paper.

Goldin, G.J. "Supervising the Multi-problem Family Worker." Unpublished paper.

Goldin, G.J.; Margolin, R.J.; Stotsky, B.A.; and Marci, J.N. *Psychodynamics and Enablement in the Rehabilitation of the Poverty-Bound Client.* Heath Lexington Books: Lexington, Mass., 1970.

Goldin, G.J.; Perry, S.L.; Margolin, R.J.; Stotsky, B.A.; and Foster, J.C. *The Rehabilitation of the Young Epileptic: Dimensions and Dynamics.* Heath Lexington Books: Lexington, Mass., 1971.

Goldman, A. "Differential Effects of Social Reward and Punishment on Dependent and Dependency-anxious Schizophrenics." *Journal of Abnormal Psychology*, 1965, 70, 412-418.

Goldstein, G. and Chotlos, J. "Dependency and Brain Damage in Alcoholics." *Perceptual and Motor Skills*, 1965, 21, 135-150.

Goldstein, G. and Chotlos, J.W. "Stability of Field Dependence in Chronic Alcoholic Patients." *Journal of Abnormal Psychology*, 1966, 71 (6), 420.

Goldstein, G.; Neuringer, C.; and Klappersack, B. "Cognitive, Perceptual, and Motor Aspects of Field Dependence in Alcoholics." *Journal of Genetic Psychology*, 1970, 117 (2), 253-266.

Goldstein, G.; Neuringer, C.; Reiff, Carolyn; and Shelly, Carolyn H. "Generalizability of Field Dependency in Alcoholics." *Journal of Consulting and Clinical Psychology*, 1968, 32 (5, Pt. 1), 560-564.

Golightly, Carole; Nelson, D.; & Johnson, J. "Children's Dependency Scale." *Developmental Psychology*, 1970, 3 (1), 114-118.

Goodman, J.S. and Buchheimer, A. "The Counselor as Knower." *Proceedings of the 74th Annual Convention of the American Psychological Association*, 1966, 303-304.

Goodman, N. "The Adolescent with a Communication Impairment." *Social Casework*, 1964, 25 (2), 46.

Gordon, B. "An Experimental Study of Dependence-independence in a Social and a Laboratory Setting." University of Southern California, 1953. Unpublished doctoral dissertation.

Gordon, O.; Brayer, R.; and Tikofsky, R. "Personality Variables and the Perception of Embedded Figures." *Perceptual & Motor Skills*, 1961, 12, 195-202.

Green, E.B. "Dependent Behavior in the Blind Adult." *Dissertation Abstracts*, 1966, 27 (5-B), 1606-1607.

Greenberg, H.R. "Transactions of a Hair-pulling Symbiosis." *Psychiatric Quarterly*, 1969, 43 (4), 662-674.

Greenblatt, M.; York, R.; and Brown, E.L. *From Custodial to Therapeutic Patient Care in Mental Hospitals: Explorations in Social Treatment.* Russel Sage Foundation, 1955.

Greenwald, E.R. "Perceptual Style in Relation to Role Choices and Motivational Variables." *Dissertation Abstracts*, 1968, 29 (6-B), 2192.

Groden, G. "The Performance of Alcoholics on the Hidden Figures and the Trail Making Tests." *Dissertation Abstracts International*, 1970, 31 (1-B), 394.

Grossman, B.D. "Parental Warmth, Child Dependency and Responsiveness to Social Reinforcement." *Dissertation Abstracts*, 1965, 26, 492.

Gruenfeld, L.W. and Weissenberg, P. "Field Independence and Articulation of Sources of Job Satisfaction." *Journal of Applied Psychology*, 1970, 54 (5), 424-426.

Gurel, Lee and Davis, J.E. "A Survey of Self-Care Dependency in Psychiatric Patients." *Hospital & Community Psychiatry*, 1967, 18 (5), 135-138.

Harano, R.M. "Relationship of Field Dependence and Motor-vehicle-accident Involvement." *Perceptual and Motor Skills*, 1970, 31 (1), 272-274.

Hare, A.; Borgatta, E.F.; and Bales, R.F. *Small Groups: Studies in Social Interaction.* New York: Knopf and Co., 1955.

Harlem Youth Opportunities Unlimited, Inc. *Youth in the Ghetto: A Study of*

Consequence of Powerlessness and a Blueprint for Change. New York, 1964, 607.

Harlow, H.F. "The Nature of Love." *American Psychologist*, 1958, 13, 673-685.

Harrison,L. "The Relationship Between Ordinal Position and Dependency, Dominance, Affiliation, Affection, and Task Orientation." *Dissertation Abstracts*, 1964, 26, 3688.

Hartup, W.W. "Nurturance and Nurturance-withdrawal in Relation to the Dependency Behavior of Preschool Children." *Child Development*, 1958, 29 (2), 191-201.

Hartup, W.W. and Keller, E.D. "Nurturance in Preschool Children and its Relation to Dependency." *Child Development*, 1960, 31, 681-689.

Hartzell, J.P. "A Preliminary Study of Nurturant and/or Aggressive Therapists' Responsiveness to Expressions of Dependency and Hostility in the Initial Phase of Psychotherapy." *Dissertation Abstracts*, 1967, 28 (3-B), 1195-1196.

Haug, M.R. and Sussman, M.B. "Professional Autonomy and the Revolt of the Client." *Social Problems*, 1969, 17 (2), 153-161.

Hauk, Mary W. "Effects of Maternal Attitudes, Field Dependence, and Curiosity on Weight and Volume Conservation in Children." *Dissertation Abstracts*, 1967, 28 (6-B), 2642.

Havens, L.M. "Dependence: Definition and Strategies." In *Report of a Dependency and Motivation Workshop*, edited by R.J. Margolin, and F.L. Hurwitz. Boston: Northeastern University, 1963.

Heathers, G. "Acquiring Dependence and Independence: A Theoretical Orientation." *Journal of Genetic Psychology*, 1955, 87, 277-291.

Heilbrun, A.B. Jr. "Counseling Readiness and the Problem-solving Behavior of Clients." *Journal of Consulting and Clinical Psychology*, 1968, 32 (4), 369-399.

Heilbrun, A.B. Jr. "Toward Resolution of the Dependency-premature Termination Paradox for Females in Psychotherapy." *Journal of Consulting and Clinical Psychology*, 1970, 34 (3), 382-386.

Heller, K. and Goldstein, A.P. "Client Dependency and Therapist Expectancy as Relationship Maintaining Variables in Psychotherapy." *Journal of Consulting Psychology*, 1961, 25, 371-375.

Heller, K.; Myers, R.A.; and Kline, L.V. "Interviewer Behavior as a Function of Standardized Client Roles." *Journal of Consulting Psychology*, 1963, 27 (2), 117-122.

Hirsch, I.R. and Singer, E. "Adolescent Dependence and Rebelliousness" (abstract). *American Psychologist*, 1961, 16, 353.

Hoffman, H.A. and Baer, P.N. "Gingival Mutilation in Children." *Psychiatry*, 1968, 31 (4), 380-386.

Hollingshead, H.E. and Redlich, O.G. *Social Class and Mental Illness: A Community Study*. New York: Wiley, 1958.

Horney, Karen. *New Ways in Psychoanalysis*. New York: W.W. Norton and Co., 1939.

Houts, P.S.; MacIntosh, Shirley; and Moos, R.H. "Patient-therapist Interdependence: Cognitive and Behavioral." *Journal of Consulting and Clinical Psychology*, 1969, 33 (1), 40-45.

Hughes, Rosalie and Reuder, Mary E. "Estimate of Psychological Time Among Obese and Nonobese Women." *Journal of Psychology*, 1968, 70 (2), 213-219.

Hurvitch, M.S. "The Experimental Arousal of Dependency Motivation." *Dissertation Abstracts*, 1960, 21, 970.

Ihilevich, D. "The Relationship of Defense Mechanisms to Field Dependence-independence." *Dissertation Abstracts*, 1968, 29 (5-B), 1843-1844.

Jacobson, E.A. "A Comparison of the Effects of Instructions and Models upon Interview Behavior of High-dependent and Low-dependent Subjects." *Dissertation Abstracts,* 1969, 29(9-B), 3485.

Jacobson, G.R. "Effect of Brief Sensory Deprivation on Field Dependence." *Journal of Abnormal Psychology*, 1966, 71(2), 115-118.

Jacobson, G.R. "Reduction of Field Dependence in Chronic Alcoholic Patients." *Journal of Abnormal Psychology*, 1968, 73(6), 547-549.

Jacobson, G.R.; Pisani, V.D.; and Berenbaum, H.L. "Temporal Stability of Field Dependence among Hospitalized Alcoholics." *Journal of Abnormal Psychology*, 1970, 76(1), 10-12.

Jakubczak, L.F. and Walters, R.H. "Suggestibility as Dependent Behavior." *Journal of Abnormal and Social Psychology*, 1959, 102-107.

Jamison, Kay and Comrey, A.L. "Further Study of Dependence as a Personality Factor." *Psychological Reports*, 1968, 22(1), 239-242.

Jaynes, J. "Imprinting, the Interaction of Learned and Innate Behavior. I. Development and Generalization." *Journal of Comparative and Physiological Psychology*, 1956, 49, 201-206.

Jaynes, J. "Imprinting, the Interaction of Learned and Innate Behavior: II. The Critical Period." *Journal of Comparative and Physiological Psychology*, 1957, 50, 6-10.

Jenson, G.D.; Bobbitt, R.A.; and Gordon, B.N. "Sex Differences in the Development of Independence of Infant Monkeys." *Behavior*, 1968, 30 (1), 1-14.

Jones, E. *Papers on Psychoanalysis*. Boston: Beacon Press, 1961.

Jones, E.; Jones, R.; and Gergen, K. "Some Conditions Affecting the Evaluation of a Conformist." *Journal of Personality*, 1963, 31, 270-288.

Jones, M. *The Therapeutic Community: A New Treatment in Psychiatry*. New York: Basic Books, 1953.

Kagan, Jerome and Moss, Howard A. "The Stability of Passive and Dependent Behavior from Childhood Through Adulthood." *Child Development*, 1960, 31, 577-591.

Kagan, J. and Mussen, P.H. "Dependency Themes on TAT and Group Conformity." *Journal of Consulting Psychology*, 1956, 20, 29-32.

Kalish, Richard A. (Ed.). *The Dependencies of Old People*. Ann Arbor, Michigan: University of Michigan, Institute of Gerontology, 1969, 106.

Karp, Stephen A. "Field Dependence and Occupational Activity in the Aged." *Perceptual and Motor Skills*, 1967, 24(2), 603-609.

Karp, S.A.; Kissen, B.; and Hustmyer, F.E. "Field Dependence as a Predictor of Alcohol Therapy Dropouts." *Journal of Nervous and Mental Disease*, 1970, 150 (1), 77-83.

Karp, S.A. and Konstadt, N.L. "Alcoholism and Psychological Differentiation: Long-range Effect of Heavy Drinking on Field Dependence." *Journal of Nervous and Mental Disease*, 1965, 140, 412-416.

Karp, S.A. and Pardes, M.D. "Psychological Differentiation in Obese Women." *Psychosomatic Medicine*, 1965, 27, 238-244.

Karp, S.A.; Silberman, L.; and Winters, S. "Psychological Differentiation and Socioeconomic Status." *Perceptual and Motor Skills*, 1969, 28 (1), 55-60.

Karp, S.A.; Witkin, H.A.; and Goodenough, D.R. "Alcoholism and Psychological Differentiation: Effect of Alcohol on Field Dependence." *Journal of Abnormal Psychology*, 1965, 70, 262-265.

Kasl, S.V.; Sampson, E.E.; and French, J.R., Jr. "The Development of a Projective Measure of the Need for Independence: A Theoretical Statement and Some Preliminary Evidence." *Journal of Personality*, 1959, 49, 243-248.

Klappersack, B. "Sources of Field Dependency in Alcoholics." *Dissertation Abstracts*, 1968, 29 (6-B), 2203.

Konstadt, N. and Forman, E. "Field Dependence and External Directedness." *Journal of Personality and Social Psychology*, 1965, 1, 490-493.

Krause, E.A. "Dependency and the Blind: Family vs. Therapeutic Work Setting." *New Outlook for the Blind*, 1962, 56, 353-357.

Kristofferson, Marianne W. "Effect of Alcohol on Perceptual Field Dependence." *Journal of Abnormal Psychology*, 1968, 73 (4), 387-391.

Kuenzli, A.E. "Preferences for High and Low Structure Among Prospective Teachers." *Journal of Social Psychology*, 1959, 49, 243-248.

Kutner, B. "Modes of Treating the Chronically Ill." In *Jewish Hospital of St. Louis: Symposium on Results in Long Term Care*, 1966, Pp. 40-57.

Lahtinen, P.M. "The Effect of Rejection and Failure on Children's Dependency." *Dissertation Abstracts*, 1964, 25, 3688-3689.

Lansky, L.M. and McKay, G. "Independence, Dependence, Manifest & Latent Masculinity-Femininity: Some Complex Relationships Among Four Complex Variables." *Psychological Reports*, 1969, 24 (1), 263-268.

Lapidus, Leah B. "Cognitive Control, Parental Practices, and Contemporary Social Problems." *Proceedings of the Annual Convention of the American Psychological Association*, 1970, 5 (Pt. 1), 427-428.

Lawrence, G.L. "Behaviors and Attitudes of College Females Differing in Parent Identification." *Dissertation Abstracts International*, 1969, 30 (3-B), 1362.

League, B.J. and Jackson, D.N. "Activity and Passivity as Correlates of Field-Independence." *Perceptual and Motor Skills*, 1961, 12, 291-298.

Lederman, S. "A Study of the Relationship Between Parents' Self Described

Dependency Attitudes, Expectation for Achievement in Their Children, and Observed Dependency Behavior in Their Children." *Dissertation Abstracts*, 1964, 25, 3676.

Lennard, H.L. and Bernstein, A. *The Anatomy of Psychotherapy*. New York: Columbia University Press, 1960.

Lester, David. "Resentment and Dependency in the Suicidal Individual." *Journal of General Psychology*, 1969, 81 (1), 137-145.

Levinson, Boris M. "Field Dependence in Homeless Men." *Journal of Clinical Psychology*, 1967, 23 (2), 152-154.

Levinson, H. *Men, Management and Mental Health*. Cambridge: Harvard University Press, 1962.

Levinson, P. "Chronic Dependency: A Conceptual Analysis." *Social Service Review*, 1964, 38(4).

Levitt, E.E.; Lubin, B.; and Zuckerman, M.A. "A Simplified Method of Scoring Rorschach for Dependency." *Journal of Projective Techniques*, 1962, 26, 234-236.

Levy, L. "A Study of Some Personality Attributes of Independents and Conformers." *Dissertation Abstracts*, 1959, 19, 1823.

Lindberg, Ruth E. "Hard to Reach: Client or Casework Agency?" *Social Work*, 1958, 3, 23-29.

Long, Barbara H.; Henderson, E.H.; and Ziller, R.C. "Developmental Changes in the Self-Concept During Middle Childhood." *Merrill-Palmer Quarterly*, 1967, 13 (3), 201-215.

Lorenz, K. (1935). "Companionship in Bird Life." In C.H. Schiller (Ed.) *Instinctive Behavior*. New York: International Universities Press, 1957. Pp. 83-116.

Lovinger, S.L. "The Interplay of Specific Ego Functions in Six Year Old Children." *Dissertation Abstracts*, 1968, 28 (11-B), 4760.

Lower, R.B. "Psychotherapy of Neurotic Dependency." *American Journal of Psychiatry*, 1967, 124 (4), 514-519.

Ludwig, E.G. and Adams, Shirley D. "Patient Cooperation in a Rehabilitation Center: Assumption of the Client Role." *Journal of Health and Social Behavior*, 1968, 9 (4), 328-336.

Ludwig, E.G. and Collette, J. "Dependency, Social Isolation and Mental Health in a Disabled Population." *Social Psychiatry*, 1970, 5 (2), 92-95.

Lynn, D.B. "Curvilinear Relation Between Cognitive Functioning and Distance of Child from Parent of the Same Sex." *Psychological Review*, 1969, 76 (2), 236-240.

Maier, H.W. "Adolescenthood." *Social Casework*, 1965, 44 (1), 3-9.

Margolin, R.J. "Criteria for Use of Directive Counseling Techniques." Unpublished paper.

Margolin, R.J. "The Failure Syndrome and Its Prevention in the Rehabilitation of the Mental Patient." *Rehabilitation Record*, 1963, 4, 34-39.

Margolin, R.J. "Member-Employee Program: New Hope for the Mentally Ill." *American Archives of Rehabilitation Therapy*, 1955, 3, 69-81.

Margolin, R.J. and Hurwitz, F.L. "The Nursing Home Administrator and Mental Health Practices in Nursing Homes." *Nursing Homes*, 1962, 11, 13-15.

Margolin, R.J. and Goldin, G.J. (Eds.) *Research Utilization Conference on Rehabilitation in Poverty Settings*, Northeastern Studies in Vocational Rehabilitation, May, 1969.

Marlow, David. "Some Psychological Correlates of Field-Independence." *Journal of Consulting Psychology*, 1958, 22, 334.

Marshall, H.R. and McCandless, B.R. "Relation Between Dependence on Adults and Social Acceptance by Peers." *Child Development*, 1957, 28, 413-419.

Marshall, S. "Personality Correlates of Peptic Ulcer Patients." *Journal of Consulting Psychology*, 1960, 24, 218-223.

Maslow, A.H. *Motivation and Personality*. New York: Harper and Bros., 1954.

McAlister, Irma R. "Interference, Immoderation, Inconsistency, and Dependency: Differences in the Behavior of Mothers Toward First and Later Born Children." *Dissertation Abstracts*, 1965, 26 (5), 2904-2905.

McBride, J.W.; Eisenman, R.; and Platt, J.J. "Dependence, Independence, Symbiosis, and Therapy." *Psychology*, 1970, 7 (3), 7-14.

McCord, W.; McCord, J.; and Verden, P. "Familial and Behavioral Correlates of Dependency in Male Children." *Child Development*, 1962, 33, 313-326.

McNair, D.M.; Callahan, D.M. and Lorr, M. "Therapist "Type" and Patient Response to Psychotherapy." *Journal of Consulting Psychology*, 1962, 26, 425-429.

McPhee, W.M.; Griffiths, K.A.; and Magleby, F.L. *Adjustment of Vocational Rehabilitation Clients*. U.S. Dept. of Health, Education, and Welfare, Vocational Rehabilitation Administration, Sept., 1963.

Meinhardt, K. and Robinson, H.A. "Stokes-Adams Syndrome Precipitated by Emotional Stress: Report of a Case." *Psychosomatic Medicine*, 1962, 24, 325-330.

Mendelson, J.; Wexler, D.; Leiderman, P.N.; and Solomon, P.A. "A Study of Addiction to Non-Ethyl Alcohols and Other Poisonous Compounds." *Quarterly Journal of Studies on Alcohol*, 1957, 18, 561-580.

Merenda, P.F.; Clark, W.V.; and Kessler, S. "AVA and the Kessler PD Scale as Measures of Passive-Dependency." *Journal of Clinical Psychology*, 1960, 16, 338-341.

Merton, R.K. *Social Theory and Social Structure*. Glencoe, Ill.: Free Press, 1957.

Messick, S. and Damarin, F. "Cognitive Styles and Memory for Faces." *Journal of Abnormal & Social Psychology*, 1964, 69, 313-318.

Meyer, Rose. "Dependency as an Asset in the Rehabilitation Process." *Rehabilitation Literature*, 1964, 25, 290-298.

Miller, J.R. and Paul, H.A. "Independence Programming Among Institutionalized Retarded Young Adults: An Anecdote and Comment." *Training School Bulletin*, 1970, 67 (2), 73-77.

Miller, W.B. "Focal Concerns of Lower Class Culture." Excerpted from "Lower

Class Culture as a Generating Milieu of Gang Delinquency." *Journal of Social Issues*, 1958, 14, 5-19.

Moore, James E. "Antecedents of Dependency and Autonomy in Young Children." *Dissertation Abstracts*, 1965, 26 (3), 1766.

Mosey, Ann. "Dependency and Integrative Skill as They Relate to Affinity For and Acceptance by an Assigned Group." *Dissertation Abstracts*, 1968, 29 (2-A), 483.

Mowrer, O.H. *Learning Theory and Behavior*. New York: Wiley, 1960.

Munt, Janet S. "Fear of Dependency: A Factor in Casework with Alcoholics." *Social Work*, 1960, 5 (1), 27-32.

Murillo, Nathan. "Conceptual Approaches to Dependency Assessment." *Dissertation Abstracts*, 1965, 26 (2), 1172-1173.

Murphy, E.B. et al., "Development of Autonomy and Parent-Child Interaction in Late Adolescence." *American Journal of Orthopsychiatry*, 1963, 33, 643-652.

Murray, H.A., Jr. *Explorations in Personality*. New York: Oxford University Press, 1938.

Navran, L. "A Rationally Derived MMPI Scale to Measure Dependency." *Journal of Consulting Psychology*, 1954, 18, 192.

Naylor, H.G. "The Relationship of Dependency Behavior to Intellectual Problem Solving." *Dissertation Abstracts*, 1965, 16, 577.

Nelson, J.W. "Dependency as a Construct: An Evaluation and Some Data." *Dissertation Abstracts*, 1959, 19, 2149.

Newcomer, R.A. "The Effects of Induced Dependency Stress and Dependency Striving on Children's Ability to Perform on Learning Tasks Which Vary in Cognitive Complexity." *Dissertation Abstracts*, 1968, 28 (10-B), 4285.

Nichols, C. and Bogdonoff, M. "Programming the Care of the Chronically Ill." *New England Journal of Medicine*, 1962, 266, 867-870.

Olshansky, S. and Margolin, R.J. "Rehabilitation as a Dynamic Interaction of Systems." *Journal of Rehabilitation*, May, 1963.

Orlando, Nita E. "Verbal Conditioning of Dependence-Independence in Domiciled Veterans." *Dissertation Abstracts*, 1969, 29 (7-B), 2639.

Parens, H. and Saul, L.J. *Dependence in Man: A Psychoanalytic Study*. New York: International Universities Press, Inc., 1971.

Parsons, T. "Social Structure and Dynamic Process: The Case of Modern Medical Practice." In *The Social System*. New York: Free Press, 1965.

Pearl, A. and Reissman, F. *New Careers for the Poor*. New York: Free Press, 1965.

Peffer, P.A. "Motivation of the Chronic Mental Patient." *American Journal of Psychiatry*, 1956, 113, 55-59.

Peffer, P.A. et al., (Eds.). *Member-Employee Program: A New Approach to the Rehabilitation of the Chronic Mental Patient*. Brockton, Mass., V.A. Hospital, 1957.

Phares, L.G. "Interpersonal Consequences of Social Power and Dependence." *Dissertation Abstracts*, 1965, 25, 4284-4285.

Perry, S.L. et al., *The Rehabilitation of the Alcohol Dependent: An Exploratory Study*. Heath Lexington Books: Lexington, Mass., 1970.

Pollack, I.W. and Kiev, A. "Spatial Orientation and Psychotherapy: An Experimental Study of Perception." *Journal of Nervous and Mental Disease*, 1963, 137, 93-97.

Potanin, N. "Perceptual Preferences as a Function of Personality Variables Under Normal and Stressful Conditions." *Journal of Abnormal and Social Psychology*, 1959, 59, 108-112.

Poussaint, A.F. "Communication With The Poor." In Margolin, R.J. and Goldin, G.J. (Eds.) *Research Utilization Conference on Rehabilitation in Poverty Settings*, Northeastern Studies in Vocational Rehabilitation, May, 1969.

Poverty Soviets. *The National Review*, 1965, 17, 907-8.

Powell, B.J. "Role of Verbal Intelligence in the Field Approach of Selected Groups of Psychotics." *Journal of Abnormal Psychology*, 1970, 76 (1), 47-49.

Pruitt, W.A. and Van de Castle, K.L. "Dependency Measures and Welfare Chronicity." *Journal of Consulting Psychology*, 1962, 26, 559-560.

Reisman, D. *The Lonely Crowd*. New Haven, Conn.: Yale University Press, 1950.

Reissman, F. "Are the Deprived Non-verbal?" In F. Reissman, J. Cohen, and A. Pearl (Eds.) *Mental Health of the Poor*. Glencoe, Ill.: Free Press, 1964. Pp. 188-193.

Renear, K.R. "Field Dependence and Parole Success." *Dissertation Abstracts International*, 1970, 30 (12-B), 5678.

Reppen, J. "Field Articulation and Socio-Economic and Rural-Urban Variables." *Dissertation Abstracts*, 1967, 28 (3-B), 1173.

Rhodes, R.J. and Yorioka, G.N. "Dependency Among Alcoholic and Nonalcoholic Institutionalized Patients." *Psychological Reports*, 1968, 22 (3, Pt. 2), 1343-1344.

Riemer, H.H. "Relationship of Cognitive Style and Reinforcement Learning in Counseling." *Dissertation Abstracts*, 1968, 28 (12-B), 5211.

Robbins, P.R. "Personality and Psychosomatic Illness: A Selective Review of Research." *Genetic Psychology Monographs*, 1969, 80 (1), 51-90.

Rodman, H. "The Lower Class Value Stretch." In L.A. Ferman; J.L. Kornbluh; and A. Haber (Eds.) *Poverty in America*. Ann Arbor: University of Michigan Press, 1965. Pp. 276-285.

Rosenthal, Miram K. "The Generalization of Dependency Behavior from Mother to Stranger." *Dissertation Abstracts*, 1965, 26, 6841.

Rothberg, June S. "Dependency and Anxiety in Male Patients Following Surgery: An Investigation of the Relationship Between Dependence, Anxiety, and Physical Manifestations of Recovery Following Surgery in Male Patients." *Dissertation Abstracts*, 1966, 27 (2-B), 525-526.

Rottschaffer, R.H. "Client Dependency in Relation to Counselor Style and Induced Client Set." *Dissertation Abstracts*, 1961, 22, 645-646.

Rudin, S.A. "Figure-Ground Differentiation Under Different Perceptual Sets." *Perceptual and Motor Skills*, 1968, 27 (1), 71-77.

Ruma, S.J. "A Multimethod Study of Developmental Differences in Adolescents with Functional and Organic Complaints." *Dissertation Abstracts*, 1967, 27 (11-B), 4134.

Sadoff, R.L. and Collins, D.J. "Passive Dependency in Stutterers." *American Journal of Psychiatry*, 1967, 30 (1), 50-63.

Santrock, J.W. "Paternal Absence, Sex Typing, and Identification." *Developmental Psychology*, 1970, 2 (2), 264-272.

Santrock, J.W. and Wohlford, P. "Effects of Father Absence: Influence of the Reason For and the Onset of the Absence." *Proceedings of the Annual Convention of the American Psychological Association*, 1970, 5 (Pt. 1), 265-266.

Scallon, R.J. and Herron, W.G. "Field Articulation of Enuretic Boys and Their Mothers." *Perceptual & Motor Skills*, 1969, 28 (2), 407-413.

Schachter, S. *The Psychology of Affiliation.* Stanford University Press, California, 1959.

Schapira, H.T. "Psychotherapy Termination as a Group Experience with Hospitalized Psychiatric Patients." *Psychotherapy: Theory, Research & Practice*, 1970, 7 (3), 155-160.

Schellenberg, J.A. "Dependency and Cooperation." *Sociometry*, 1965, 28, 158-172.

Schopler, J. and Bateson, N. "The Power of Dependency." *Journal of Personality & Social Psychology*, 1965, 2, 247-254.

Schopler, J. and Mathews, M.W. "The Influence of the Perceived Causal Locus of Partner's Dependence on the Use of Interpersonal Power." *Journal of Personality & Social Psychology*, 1965, 2, 609-612.

Schuldt, W.J. "Psychotherapists' Approach-Avoidance Responses and Clients' Expressions of Dependency." *Journal of Counseling Psychology*, 1966, 13, 178-183.

Schuldt, W.J. "Reinforcement on Elicitation Effects of Approach Responses by Psychotherapists." *Journal of Counseling Psychology*, 1968, 15 (3), 295-296.

Schwaab, E. "Dependency Factors in Relation to Recall of Dependency Material." Boston University Dissertation, 1959.

Schwartz, D.W. and Karp, A. "Field Dependence in a Geriatric Population." *Perceptual & Motor Skills*, 1967, 24 (2), 495-504.

Scodel, A. "Heterosexual Somatic Preferences and Fantasy Dependency." *Journal of Consulting Psychology*, 1957, 21, 371-374.

Scott, Bertha H. "Tensions Linked With Emphysema." *American Journal of Nursing, 1969, 69 (3), 538-540.*

Sears, R.R. "Dependency Motivation." In M.R. Jones (Ed.). *Nebraska Symposium on Motivation*. Lincoln, Nebraska: University of Nebraska Press, 1963. Pp. 25, 51-53.

Sherman, R.C. and Smith, Frances. "Sex Differences in Cue Dependency as a Function of Socialization Environment." *Perceptual & Motor Skills*, 1967, 24 (2), 599-602.

Shows, W.D. and Carson, R.C. "The A-B Therapist 'Type' Distinction and Spatial Orientation: Replication and Extension." *Journal of nervous and mental Disease*, 1965, 141, 456-462.

Siddigi, Ismat B. "Dependency and Hostility Responses of the Counselee as related to Changes in his Sociometric Status." *Dissertation Abstracts*, 1968, 28 (10-A) 3978.

Silberman, C.E. "Up from Apathy—the Woodlawn Experiment." *Commentary*, 1964, 37, 51-58.

Silverstone, S. and Kissin, B. "Field Dependence in Essential Hypertension and Peptic Ulcer." *Journal of Psychosomatic Research*, 1968, 12 (2), 157-161.

Sistrunk, F. "Conditioning and Extinction of Conformity Behavior." *Psychonomic Science*, 1969, 17 (4), 255-256.

Snyder, W.U. *Dependency in Psychotherapy*. New York: The MacMillan Co., 1963.

Speer, D.C. "Concurrent Schedules of Reinforcement, Social Reinforcement, and Dependent Behavior Among Four Year Old Children." *Dissertation Abstracts*, 1967, 27 (12-B), 4586-4587.

Speisman, J.C. and Singer, M.T. "Rorschach Content Correlates in Five Groups With Organic Pathology." *Journal of Projective Techniques*, 1961, 25, 356-359.

Spencer, G. "Social Research: The Role It Plays in a Demonstration Project." *Rehabilitation Literature*, 1966, 27, 76-78, 95.

Spencer, G. *Structure and Dynamics of Social Intervention*. Lexington, Mass.: Heath Lexington Books, 1970.

Spiegel, D.E. and Litrownik, Allan J. "The Effects of Dependency and Self-Assertiveness of Schizophrenic Patients on Susceptibility to Group Influence in Perceptual Tasks." *Journal of Clinical Psychology*, 1968, 24 (1), 12-16.

Stanton, A.H. and Schwartz, U.S. *The Mental Hospital: A Study of Institutional Participation in Psychiatric Illness and Treatment*. New York: Basic Books, 1958.

Stewart, D.J. and Resnick, J.H. "Verbal Conditioning and Dependency Behavior in Delinquents." *Journal of Abnormal and Social Psychology*, 1970, 73 (3, Pt. 1), 357-377.

Stewart, R.H. "Birth Order and Dependency." *Journal of Personality and Social Psychology*, 1967, 6 (2), 192-4.

"Strength Through Misery." *Time*, 1965, 87, 28-29.

Stotsky, B.A. "Social Psychological Factors in Dependency." *Rehabilitation Record*, 1963, 4 (4), 8-9.

Stotsky, B.A. and Margolin, R.J. "Some Reflections on Psychotherapy and Counseling For Member-Employees." In Peffer et al., (Eds.) *Member-Employee Program: A New Approach to the Rehabilitation of the Chronic Mental Patient*, Brockton, Mass.: V.A. Hospital, 1957, 183-190.

Sugarman, A.A. and Cancro, R. "Field Independence and Outcome in Schizophrenia: A U-Shaped Relationship." *Perceptual and Motor Skills*, 1968, 27 (3, Pt. 1), 1007-1013.

Sullivan, H.S. *The Interpersonal Theory of Psychiatry*. New York: Norton, 1953.

Sweeney, D.R. and Fine, B.J. "Pain Reactivity and Field Dependency." *Perceptual and Motor Skills*, 1965, 21, 757-758.

Swift, C.R.; Seidman, Frances; and Stein, H. "Adjustment Problems in Juvenile Diabetes." *Psychosomatic Medicine*, 1967, 29 (6), 555-571.

Switzer, Mary. "The Importance of Rehabilitation as a Deterrent to Dependency." *Journal of Rehabilitation*, 1963, 29 (5), 20.

Tongas, P.N. "The Effects of Dependency on Persuasibility." *Dissertation Abstracts*, 1965, 25, 5391.

Waldrop, M.F. and Bell, R.Q. "Preschool Dependent Behavior and Maternal Availability." *American Psychologist*, 1963, 18, 339. (Abstract)

Waldrop, M.F. and Bell, R.Q. "Effects of Family Size and Density on Newborn Characteristics." *American Journal of Orthopsychiatry*, 1966, 36 (3), 544-550.

Wallach, M.A.; Kogan, N.; and Burt, R.B. "Group Risk Taking and Field Independence of Group Members." *Sociometry*, 1967, 30 (4), 323-338.

Walters, R.H. and Foote, A. "A Study of Reinforcer Effectiveness with Children." *Merrill-Palmer Quarterly*, 1962, 8, 149-157.

Watson, B.L. "Field Dependence and Early Reading Achievement." *Dissertation Abstracts International*, 1970, 31 (2-A), 656-657.

Weiss, P. and Emmerich, W. "Dependency, Fantasy, and Group Conformity in Ulcer Patients." *Journal of Consulting Psychology*, 1962, 26, 61-64.

Wertz, C.E., Jr. "Multidimensional Analyses of Psychological Constructs." *Dissertation Abstracts*, 1961, 21, 2008.

Whitehorn, J.C. and Betz, B.J. "Further Studies of the Doctor as a Crucial Variable in the Outcome of Treatment with Schizophrenic Patients." *American Journal of Psychiatry*, 1960, 117, 215-223.

Whyte, W.H. *The Organization Man*. New York: Doubleday, 1957.

Willoughby, R.H. "Field Dependence and Locus of Control." *Perceptual & Motor Skills*, 1967, 24 (2), 671-672.

Wiltse, K.T. "The 'Hopeless' Family" *Social Work*, 1958, 3 (4), 12-22.

Winder, C.L. et al., "Dependency of Patients, Psychotherapists' Responses, and Aspects of Psychotherapy." *Journal of Consulting Psychology*, 1962, 26 (2), 129-134.

Winestine, Muriel C. "Twinship and Psychological Differentiation." *Dissertation Abstracts*, 1966, 26 (7), 4082-4083.

Winnicott, D.W. "Dependence in Infant Care, in Child Care, and in the Psychoanalytic Setting." *International Journal of Psychoanalysis*, 1963, 24, 4831-4832.

Witkin, H.A. "Individual Differences in Ease of Perception of Embedded Figures." *Journal of Personality*, 1950, 19, 1-15.

Witkin, H.A. "Psychological Differentiation and Forms of Pathology." *Journal of Abnormal Psychology*, 1965, 70 (5), 317-336.

Witkin, H.A. et al., *Psychological Differentiation*. New York: Wiley, 1962.

Witkin, H.A.; Karp, S.A.; and Goodenough, D.R. "Dependency in Alcoholics." *Quarterly Journal of Studies on Alcohol*, 1959, 20, 493-504.

Witkin, H.A.; Lewis, H.B.; and Weil, E. "Affective Reactions and Patient-Therapist Interactions Among More Differentiated and Less Differentiated Patients Early in Therapy." *Journal of Nervous and Mental Disease*, 1968, 146 (3), 193-208.

Wohlford, P. and Liberman, D. "Effect of Father Absence on Personal Time, Field Independence, and Anxiety." *Proceedings of the Annual Convention of the American Psychological Association*, 1970, 5 (Pt. 1), 263-264.

Wolkon, G.H. "Birth Order and Desire For and Participation in Psychiatric Posthospital Services." *Journal of Consulting and Clinical Psychology*, 1968, 32 (1), 42-46.

Wolkon, G.H. "Characteristics of Clients and Continuity of Care into the Community." *Community Mental Health Journal*, 1970, 6 (3), 215-221.

Wright, Beatrice A. *Physical Disability: A Psychological Approach*. New York: Harper and Row, 1960. Pp. 13-16; 303-317.

Wright, H.L., Jr. "A Clinical Study of Children Who Refuse to Talk in School." *Journal of the American Academy of Child Psychiatry*, 1968, 7 (4), 603-617.

Zola, L.K. "The Effect of Separation From Parents on the Dependency of Asthmatic and Non-Asthmatic Children." *Dissertation Abstracts*, 1967, 28 (5-B), 2152.

Zuckerman, M. "The Validity of The EPPS in the Measurement of Dependency-Rebelliousness." *Journal of Clinical Psychology*, 1958, 14, 379-382.

Zuckerman, M. and Grosz, H. "Suggestibility and Dependency." *Journal of Consulting Psychology*, 1958, 22, 328.

Zuckerman, M.; Levitt, E.E.; and Lubin, B. "Concurrent and Construct Validity of Direct and Indirect Measures of Dependency." *Journal of Consulting Psychology*, 1961, 25, 316-323.

About the Authors

George J. Goldin is director of research at the New England Rehabilitation Research Institute and professor of special education at Northeastern University, Boston, Massachusetts. He received his B.S. degree in psychology from the University of Massachusetts, his M.S. in psychiatric social work from Boston University, and his Ph.D. degree from Brandeis University. He has had extensive experience in the fields of mental health, family counseling, community planning and social welfare. His background includes positions on clinical practice, supervisory, administrative and planning levels. He is the author of numerous articles and monographs in the field of rehabilitation, the sociology of organizations and various phases of social work.

Sally Perry is a research associate at the New England Rehabilitation Research Institute. She received her B.S. and M.S. in psychology from the University of Massachusetts and has participated in a number of research studies in the areas of motivation and dependency.

The late **Reuben J. Margolin** was Chairman of the Department of Rehabilitation and Special Education and Project Director of the New England Regional Rehabilitation Research Institute which is funded by the Social and Rehabilitation Service. The Institute has as its core area the relationship of motivation to dependency in the rehabilitation of the disabled.

Prior to coming to Northeastern University, he was counseling psychologist and Director of the Member Employee Rehabilitation Work Program at the Veterans Administration Hospital in Brockton.

He was rehabilitation consultant to many agencies, including Veterans Administration, World University in Puerto Rico, Massachusetts Department of Mental Health, and Morgan Memorial. He received outstanding achievement awards from the President's Committee on Employing the Handicapped, American Association of Medical Rehabilitation Directors and Coordinators, Massachusetts Federation of Nursing Homes, and the National Conference of Christians and Jews.

He published five books and over 100 articles.

Bernard Stotsky is an M.D. whose past affiliations included Director of Psychological Services, Veterans Administration Hospital, Brockton; faculty of Boston University and Duke University Medical School. Currently a practicing psychiatrist, he is a research consultant to New England Rehabilitation Research Institute. He has published several books on geriatric psychiatry and has published widely in the field of rehabilitation, psychology, and medicine.

139